READER'S DIGEST BASIC G

Make your own Bread, Cakes and Pastry

Contents

THE TEXT AND ILLUSTRATIONS IN THIS BOOK
ARE TAKEN FROM 'THE COOKERY YEAR'
PUBLISHED BY THE READER'S DIGEST ASSOCIATION LIMITED
LONDON NEW YORK CAPE TOWN MONTREAL SYDNEY

Pastry/1

Traditional shortcrust pastry

The many different kinds of pastry which are made in Britain today have evolved over the centuries from a crude flour and water dough mixture invented by the Romans. The paste was wrapped round meat and game before roasting and was not intended to be eaten. It served only to retain the meat juices and aroma.

As time passed, the paste was enriched with fat and milk and began vaguely to resemble today's shortcrust pastry. By medieval times, pastry-making was well-established and rich-crust pastry coverings, known as coffers, became as important as the contents of the huge fruit, fish, meat and game pies they covered.

As different areas and localities developed their own puddings and pies, many pastry variations emerged from the basic fat, flour and water recipe. Perhaps the most famous of all is the 14th-century raised hot-water crust. This was indigenous to Britain and was used with meat and game pies. It was moulded from the inside with a clenched fist, in the same way as a clay pot, and then filled and baked until crisp and brown. The method is perpetuated in the Melton Mowbray pork pies.

By the 17th century both flaky and puff pastries were being used for elaborate pies, and the decorations and intricate patterns on the finished pies were works of art. Later still, continental pastry-making was added to the ever-growing number of recipes, and yet today the basic art of pastry-making is much as it has been for centuries.

Pastry is no longer used principally to retain the juices of the filling it covers. Its chief purpose is to complement the flavour of the filling and at the same time to provide a convenient casing in which anything from a steak and kidney pudding to a lemon meringue pie may be cooked. It also helps to eke out a limited amount of meat, fish, game or fruit.

Although much mystique surrounds pastry-making, there are no great secrets to guarantee instant success, for pastry-making is an art which is mastered by care, patience and practice. There are, however, a few essentials which must be observed before good results can be achieved. The kitchen, working surface and utensils should be cool, and the recipe must always be strictly adhered to, especially in regard to measurements. Pastry should be made as quickly as possible, and handling kept to a minimum. Many pastries are best rested in a cool place before they are cooked.

Shortcrust, with its variations, is probably the best known and most commonly used pastry. Next in popularity are the more robust pastries, such as suet and hot-water crust. Choux, and the flaky and rough puff pastry are slightly more difficult, while puff pastry is considered to be the hardest of all. But even with these, patience and practice can achieve splendid results.

PREPARING TRADITIONAL SHORTCRUST PASTRY

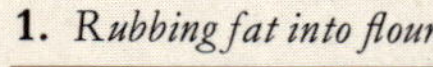

1. *Rubbing fat into flour*

2. *Mixing water into dough*

3. *Kneading dough lightly*

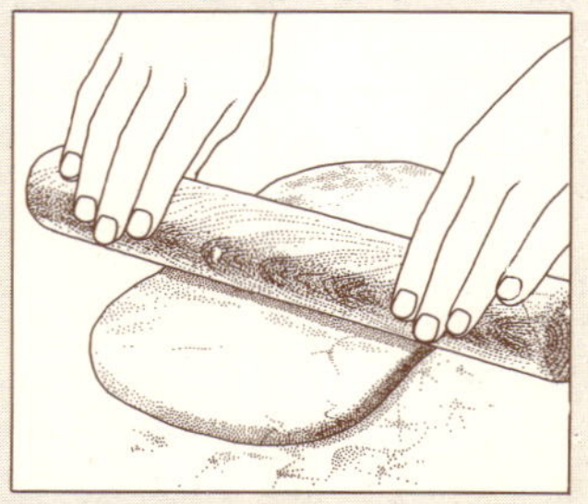

4. *Rolling out the pastry*

SHORTCRUST PASTRY

This popular and versatile pastry is used for savoury and sweet pies, tarts, flans and tartlets. It is usually made by the 'rubbing-in' method, but there are several other ways of making shortcrust. Plain flour is recommended; self-raising flour may be used, but the pastry will be more crumbly. The fat should be lard or a white vegetable fat; ideally, use equal amounts of lard and firm margarine. Margarine alone produces a yellow, firm pastry.

The standard recipe is for 8 oz. shortcrust which always means 8 oz. flour to 4 oz. fat. The amount of flour may be doubled or halved, but proportions should remain the same: half the fat to the amount of flour.

The standard recipe yields enough pastry to cover a 2 pint dish, or a 9 in. flan ring, or to line and cover a 7 in. pie plate.

The following basic shortcrust pastries may be used for both savoury and sweet pies. Enriched shortcrust pastry, however, is mainly used for flans. Shortcrust pastries are usually baked in the centre of a pre-heated oven, at 400°F (mark 6).

Traditional Shortcrust

PREPARATION TIME: *15 min.*

INGREDIENTS:
8 oz. plain flour
½ level teaspoon salt
2 oz. lard
2 oz. margarine or butter
2–3 tablespoons cold water

Sift the flour and salt into a wide bowl. Cut up the firm fats and rub them into the flour, using the tips of the fingers, until the mixture resembles fine breadcrumbs. Lift the dry mixture well out of the bowl and let it trickle back through the fingers to keep the pastry cool and light. Add the water, sprinkling it evenly over the surface (uneven addition of the water may cause blistering when the pastry is cooked). Mix the dough lightly with a round-bladed knife until it forms large lumps.

Gather the dough together with the fingers until it leaves the sides of the bowl clean. Form it into one piece and knead it lightly on a floured surface until firm and

Pastry/2

One-stage (fork) pastry

Enriched shortcrust pastry

Cheese pastry

Covering a pie dish

Preparing a double crust pie

free from cracks. Chill for 30 minutes before use.

Roll the pastry out as required, using short, light strokes and rotate the pastry regularly to keep it an even shape.

One-stage (Fork) Pastry

A shortcrust pastry using soft table margarine to give a yellow-tinted pastry with a smooth appearance and soft crumb.

PREPARATION TIME: *10 min.*

INGREDIENTS:
5 oz. soft table margarine
8 oz. plain flour
2 tablespoons water

Put the soft margarine with 2 tablespoons of flour and the water in a deep mixing bowl. Cream these ingredients with a fork until well mixed. Still using the fork, work in the remaining flour to form a manageable dough. Turn this on to a floured surface and knead lightly until smooth. Chill for 30 minutes.

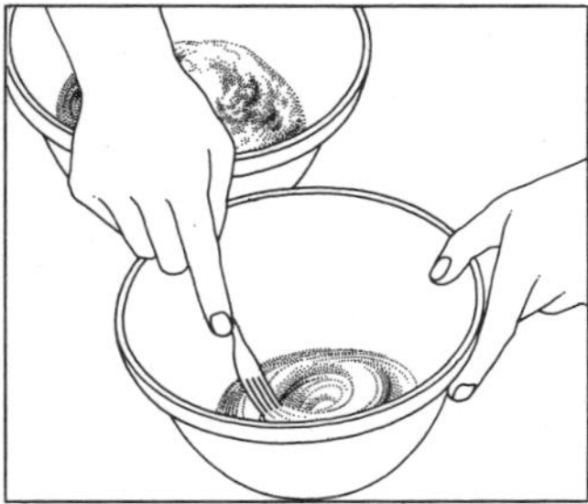

To make one-stage pastry, cream margarine with flour and water

Enriched Shortcrust Pastry

PREPARATION TIME: *10 min.*

INGREDIENTS:
5 oz. plain flour
Pinch salt
3 oz. unsalted butter or margarine
1 egg yolk
1½ level teaspoons caster sugar
3–4 teaspoons water

Sift the flour and salt into a wide bowl. Cut up the fat and rub it into the flour with the fingertips until the mixture resembles breadcrumbs. Beat the egg yolk, sugar and 2 teaspoons of water in a separate bowl and pour it into the flour mixture. Stir with a round-bladed knife, adding more water as necessary until the mixture begins to form a dough. Gather this into a ball and turn it on to a floured surface. Knead lightly.

Cheese Pastry

A shortcrust pastry ideal for cheese straws, as a crust for vegetable pies, and for flan cases.

PREPARATION TIME: *10 min.*

INGREDIENTS:
4 oz. plain flour
Salt and cayenne pepper
2 oz. butter or margarine
2 oz. Cheddar, Lancashire or Cheshire cheese
1 egg yolk
2–3 teaspoons cold water

Sift the flour, a pinch of salt and a shake of cayenne into a wide bowl. Cut up the fat and rub it into the flour with the fingertips until the mixture resembles fine breadcrumbs. Blend in the grated cheese and stir in the egg yolk mixed with 1 tablespoon of water to ensure even distribution. Add more water to give a stiff dough.

Knead the dough lightly on a floured surface, and chill.

Covering a Pie Dish

Roll out the pastry to the required thickness (no more than ¼ in. thick) and 2 in. wider than the pie dish, using the inverted dish as a guide. Cut a 1 in. wide strip from the outer edge of the pastry and place it on the moistened rim of the pie dish. Seal the strip with water where it joins and brush the whole strip with water.

Fill the pie dish and set a pie funnel in the centre; lift the remaining pastry on the rolling pin and lay it over the pie dish. Press the pastry strip and lid firmly together with the fingers. Trim any excess pastry with a knife blade held at a slight angle to the dish.

To seal the pastry edges firmly so that they do not come apart during baking, hold the knife blade horizontally towards the pie dish and make a series of shallow cuts in the pastry edges – this is known as 'knocking up'. Use the pastry trimmings to cut decorative shapes for the top of the pie. Cut a slit into the centre of the pastry for the steam to escape, and decorate the edges.

Preparing a Double Crust Pie

Divide the pastry into two portions, one slightly larger than the other. Shape the larger portion into a ball and roll it out on a lightly floured surface, to a thickness of a 10p coin. Rotate the pastry between rolls to keep the

COVERING A PIE DISH

Trim the pastry to fit the dish

Cover the filled pie dish

'Knock up' pastry edges

MAKING A DOUBLE CRUST PIE

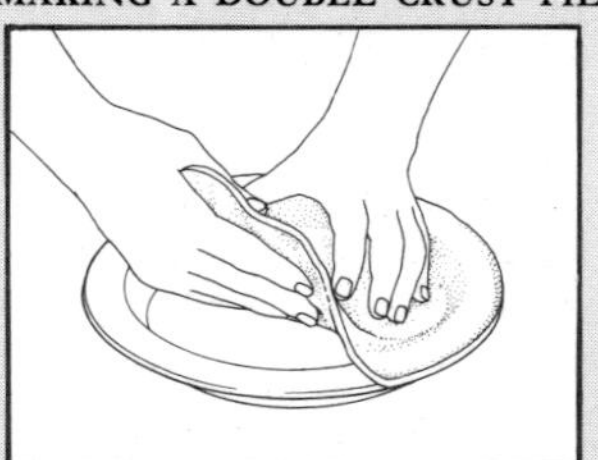

Lift pastry into pie plate

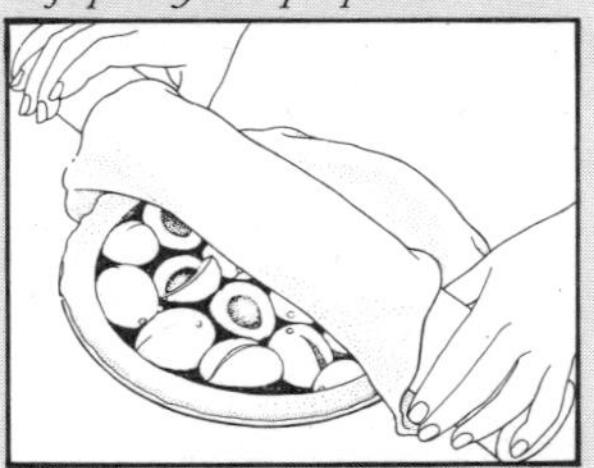

Place pastry lid in position

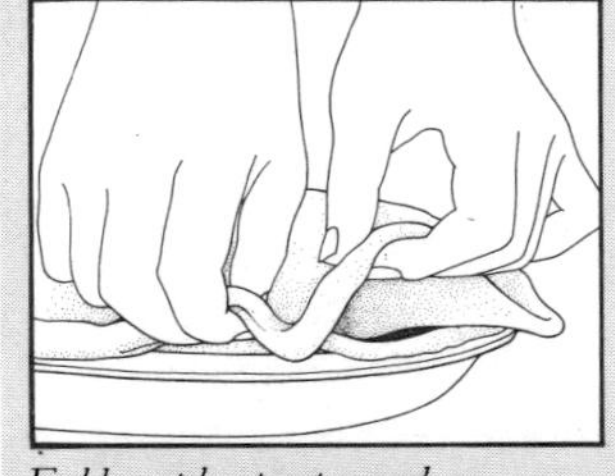

Fold surplus pastry under

Pastry/3

Lining a pie plate

Baking blind

Lining a flan ring

Lining tartlet moulds

Finishing and decorations

edge round; if the edge begins to break pinch it together with the fingers. Roll out the pastry about 1 in. wider than the inverted pie plate.

Fold the pastry in half and lift it on to the pie plate; unfold and loosely ease the pastry into position, being careful not to stretch the pastry. Put the cold filling over the pastry base, keeping it slightly domed in the centre. Roll out the remaining pastry for the lid, allowing about $\frac{1}{2}$ in. beyond the rim. Brush the edge of the pastry lining with water, then lift the lid on the rolling pin and place in position over the filling.

Seal the edges by either folding the surplus edge of the lid firmly over the rim of the lining, or by trimming the edges almost level with the plate and knocking them up with a knife. Cut a slit in the centre of the pastry lid for the steam to escape.

Lining a Pie Plate

For an open pie, roll out the pastry $\frac{1}{6}$ in. thick and about 1 in. wider than the pie plate. Lift the pastry into the plate and ease it loosely over the base and sides. Trim the pastry with scissors to $\frac{1}{2}$ in. from the plate edge, then fold the pastry under the rim of the plate. Flute the edge (see Finishing and Decorations) so that the points protrude over the plate rim and thus prevent shrinking during baking.

Baking Blind

Sometimes pastry, especially flan cases and individual tartlets, has to be baked before the filling is put in. This is known as baking blind. Line the pastry case with foil or greaseproof paper cut to shape and weigh it down with dried beans (if kept specially for this purpose, the beans can be used again and again). Bake the pastry case in the centre of a pre-

To bake blind, cover pastry with paper and weigh down with beans

heated oven at 400°F (mark 6) for 15 minutes. Remove the beans and foil and bake for a further 5–10 minutes or until the pastry is dry and lightly browned.

Alternatively, and especially for tartlets, prick the base and sides of the pastry with a fork before lining it with foil. Dried beans are not necessary if the pastry is pricked.

Flan cases and tartlet moulds should be left on a wire rack to cool and shrink slightly before being eased out of their moulds.

LINING A FLAN RING

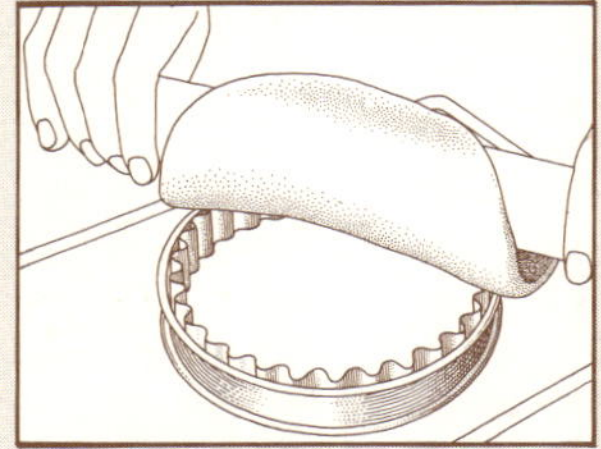

Lay pastry over flan

Press pastry into fluted ridges

Roll off surplus pastry

Lining a Flan Ring

Flans are baked in plain or fluted rings set on baking trays or in a French fluted flan tin with a loose base. Roll the pastry out as thinly as possible, $\frac{1}{8}$ in. or less, to a circle 2 in. wider than the ring. With the rolling pin, lift the pastry and lower it into the flan ring. Lift the edges carefully and press the pastry gently into shape with the fingers, taking care that no air pockets are left between the ring and the pastry. Trim the pastry in a plain ring with a knife or scissors, just above the rim, and knock up the edges. On a fluted flan ring, press the pastry against the inner fluted ring edges then use the rolling pin to cut the pastry level with the rim.

LINING TARTLET MOULDS

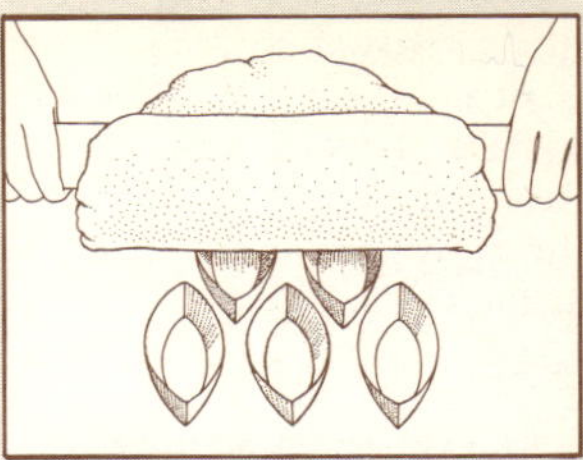

Lay pastry over the moulds

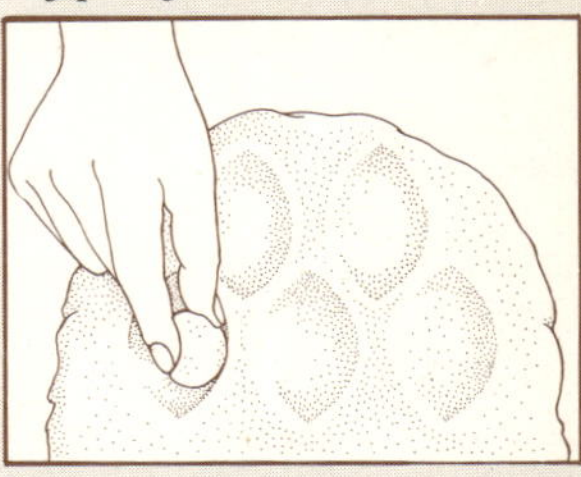

Shape moulds with pastry ball

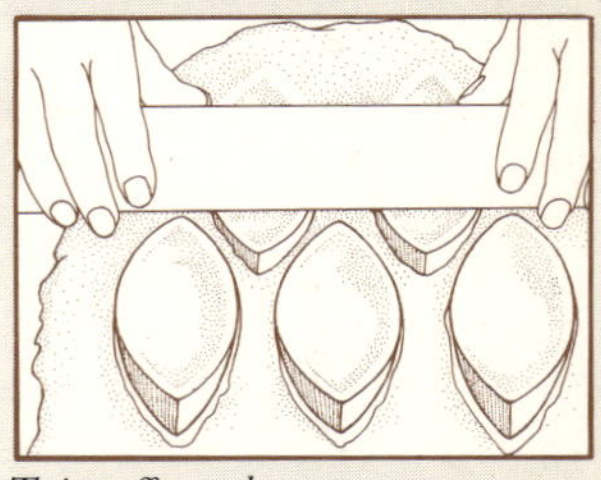

Trim off surplus pastry

Lining Tartlet Moulds

Set the small moulds closely together on a baking tray. Roll out the pastry, $\frac{1}{8}$ in. thick, to a rectangle or square large enough to cover the whole area of moulds. Lay the pastry loosely over the moulds, press it into the moulds with a small ball of pastry. Run the rolling pin over the moulds, first in one direction, then in the other, and trim off any surplus. Press the pastry into shape with the fingers and prick the bases (see Baking Blind).

To line a sheet of patty pans, use a plain or fluted cutter, $\frac{1}{2}$–$\frac{3}{4}$ in. wider than the patty, to cut out rounds from the pastry. Ease the pastry rounds into the patties and prick them with a fork.

Finishing and Decorations

The two edges of a covered pie can be finished in a number of decorative ways. To make a scalloped or fluted pattern on savoury pies, use the thumb or the back of a spoon handle to press the edges together. Alternatively, press the edges between thumb and index finger, at intervals of ½–¾ in.; draw a knife between the indentations towards the centre of the pie.

Sweet pies are usually finished with a twisted or ridged edge. Twist and slightly turn the edges together between thumb and index finger, at ½ in. intervals. Alternatively, seal the edges with the tines of a fork.

DECORATING PIE EDGES

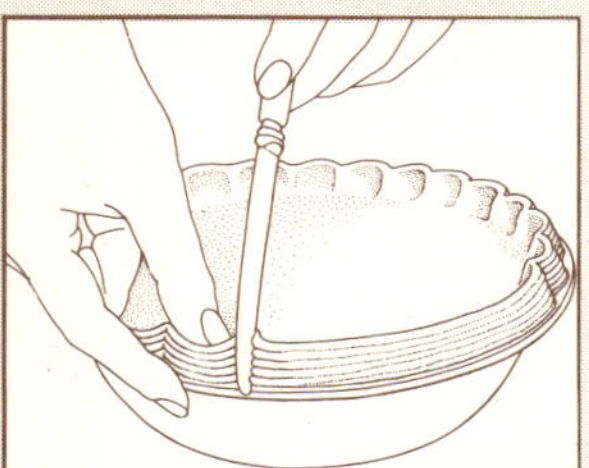

Making a scalloped pattern

Making a twisted edge

The top of a covered pie may be decorated with the pastry trimmings. Roll the pastry out thinly and cut into small shapes.

To make leaves, cut the pastry into 1–1½ in. wide strips and cut these into diamond shapes. With the back of a knife, trace the ribs.

PASTRY DECORATIONS

Pastry leaf shapes

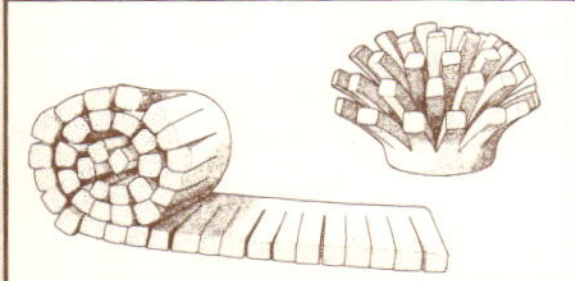

Pastry tassel

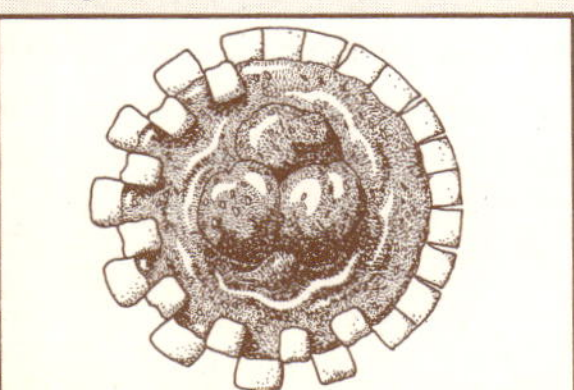

Cut edges on a flan

For a tassel, cut a 1 in. wide pastry slice about 6 in. long. Make cuts, ¾ in. long, at intervals of ¼ in., then roll up the strip, place it on the pie and open out.

Finish the edges of open flans and tarts by fluting or crimping. A simple method, using a pair of scissors, is to make cuts just over ¼ in. deep and a little over ¼ in. apart around the pastry edge. Fold alternate pieces of pastry inwards and bend the remaining pieces outwards. Or the edges can be decorated with thin pastry strips that have been twisted or braided. Moisten the pastry edge with water first.

A lattice pattern is a traditional decoration for many open flans. Cut the rolled out pastry trimmings into ½ in. wide strips (a pastry wheel gives an attractive edge) and long enough to cover the flan. Moisten the flan edges, then lay half the strips over the filling, 1 in. apart, and lay the remaining strips criss-crossing the first. Trim the strips to shape at the outer edge, or fold the pastry lining down over them for a neater finish. For a really professional touch, the pastry strips should be interwoven by laying them over the filling 1 in. apart, and a strip of pastry at a right angle across the centre. Lift alternate lengths of the first strips of pastry on one half of the tart and place a strip at right angles. Replace the top strips and repeat with the other side of the tart to complete the interwoven effect. The strips may also be twisted before being arranged in the lattice pattern.

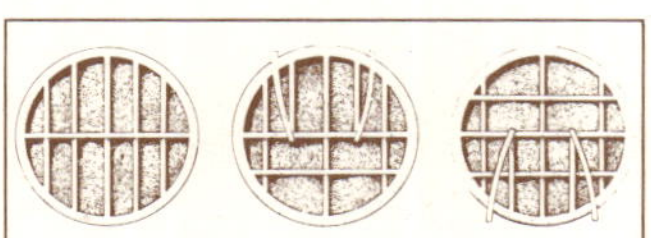

Lattice pattern: lay pastry strips over flan top; interleave crossing strips

Pies can be decorated with pastry flowers. Simple flowers are made by rolling a small piece of pastry to the size and shape of an acorn. Cut out two diamond shapes and pinch the edges to round them to a petal shape. Dampen the base of the petals and wrap around the wide base of the acorn shape. Pinch the pastry to seal the pieces together, then bend the tip of each petal slightly outwards.

More ornate flowers can be made by making a cross with a knife on a small, flattened round of pastry. Set the round on a square of dampened pastry; set this in turn on another square of dampened pastry, similar in size, to form a star pattern. Shape the corners of the squares to resemble petals. Pinch and shape each point of the central round of pastry into a petal to complete the flower.

Glazing

Brush the decorated pie or flan before baking to give a shiny golden look. Brush savoury pies with beaten whole egg or with egg yolk diluted with a little water or milk, and a pinch of salt. Glaze sweet pies with milk or egg white and dust with caster sugar.

Apple Pie

PREPARATION TIME: *20 min.*
COOKING TIME: *35 min.*

INGREDIENTS *(for 4–6):*
6–8 oz. shortcrust pastry
1½ lb. cooking apples
2–3 oz. caster or Demerara sugar
Milk

Peel and core the apples and cut them into chunky slices. Place a pie funnel in the centre of a 1½ pint pie dish, arrange half the apple slices in the dish, sprinkle over the sugar and add the remaining fruit with 3 tablespoons of water.

Cover the pie with the rolled-out pastry, decorate it and brush the top with milk. Dust with caster sugar. Make a slit in the centre of the pastry lid for the steam to escape. Set the pie on a baking tray and bake in the centre of the oven pre-heated to 400°F (mark 6) for 35–40 minutes. If the pastry browns too quickly, cover it with a double layer of moistened greaseproof paper.

For variation, the water may be replaced with orange juice and the grated rind of half an orange mixed with the sugar.

Alternatively, use 1 lb. apples and ½ lb. blackberries for the filling. Other fruits, such as halved and stoned apricots, damsons, plums and greengages, topped and tailed gooseberries and 1 in. pieces of trimmed rhubarb also make good fruit pies. For gooseberry and rhubarb pie, increase the amount of sugar to 4 oz.

Pastry/5

Cheese and onion pie

Cheese and bacon quiche

Lemon meringue pie

Duke of Cambridge tart

Mince pies

Cheese and Onion Pie

PREPARATION TIME: *30 min.*
COOKING TIME: *35 min.*

INGREDIENTS *(for 4–6)*:
8 oz. shortcrust pastry
4 large onions (approx. 1 lb.)
6–8 oz. coarsely grated mature cheese
½ level teaspoon grated nutmeg
1 level teaspoon salt
Black pepper
2 teaspoons Worcestershire sauce
Milk

Peel and quarter the onions, cook them in boiling water for about 15 minutes, or until they are just tender. Drain thoroughly in a colander, then cool slightly before chopping them roughly.

Divide the prepared pastry in two and roll out each half to fit a 7 in. pie plate. Line the plate with half the pastry and cover with half the cheese and the onions. Season with nutmeg, salt, pepper and Worcestershire sauce. Top with the remaining cheese, and cover the pie with pastry. Seal and knock up the edges. Brush with milk and make a small slit in the pastry lid. Bake in pre-heated oven, at 400°F (mark 6), for 30–35 minutes.

Cheese and Bacon Quiche

PREPARATION TIME: *30 min.*
COOKING TIME: *40 min.*

INGREDIENTS *(for 4–6)*:
6 oz. shortcrust pastry
2 oz. onion
½ oz. butter or margarine
4 oz. lean streaky bacon
4 oz. grated Cheddar cheese
2 large eggs
¼ pint milk
2 tablespoons single cream or top of the milk
Salt and black pepper
1 tablespoon freshly chopped parsley (optional)

Roll out the pastry and use it to line an 8–8½ in. flan. ring. Peel and finely chop the onion, fry it in the butter over low heat for 5 minutes until soft and transparent. Set aside. Remove the rind and gristle from the rashers and cut the bacon into small pieces. Fry until the fat runs and the bacon begins to crisp. Drain off the fat.

Mix the onion and bacon and arrange it in the flan case; cover with the cheese.

Lightly whisk the eggs with the milk and cream; add the chopped parsley and season to taste. Spoon this mixture over the flan filling and bake in the centre of a pre-heated oven, at 400°F (mark 6), for 30 minutes. Reduce the heat to 350°F (mark 4) and bake for a further 10 minutes, until the filling is set and the pastry crisp and golden brown.

Lemon Meringue Pie

PREPARATION TIME: *30 min.*
COOKING TIME: *40 min.*

INGREDIENTS *(for 4–6)*:
4 oz. shortcrust pastry
1 large thin-skinned lemon
2–3 level tablespoons granulated sugar
2 level tablespoons cornflour
2 eggs
½ oz. unsalted butter
4 oz. caster sugar

Roll out the pastry and line an 8½ in. pie plate or a 7 in. flan ring. Bake the pastry case blind in the centre of a pre-heated oven, at 400°F (mark 6) for about 15 minutes or until the pastry is crisp and golden. When cold, remove the pastry from the pie plate or ease away the flan ring.

Meanwhile, peel the rind from the lemon in thin slivers, carefully omitting all white pith. Squeeze the juice from the lemon and set it aside. Put the lemon peel, granulated sugar and ½ pint of water in a pan; cook over low heat until the sugar has dissolved, then bring this syrup to the boil. Remove the pan from the heat. Blend the cornflour in a bowl with 3 tablespoons lemon juice, then pour in the syrup through a strainer, stirring thoroughly. Separate the eggs, and beat in the egg yolks, one at a time, together with the butter. The mixture should be thick enough to coat the back of a wooden spoon; otherwise return it to the pan and cook for a few minutes without boiling. Spoon the lemon mixture into the cooked pastry case, set on a baking tray.

Whisk the egg whites until stiff, then add half the caster sugar and continue whisking until the meringue holds its shape and stands in soft peaks. Fold in all but 1 teaspoon of the remaining sugar, using a metal spoon.

Pile the meringue over the lemon filling; spread it from the edge towards the centre, making sure that the meringue joins the pastry edge to prevent the meringue 'weeping'. Sprinkle the meringue with the remaining sugar. Reduce the heat to 300°F (mark 2) and bake the pie in the centre of the oven for 20–30 minutes, or until the meringue is crisp. Serve the pie warm, rather than hot or cold.

Duke of Cambridge Tart

PREPARATION TIME: *15 min.*
COOKING TIME: *40 min.*

INGREDIENTS *(for 4)*:
4 oz. shortcrust pastry
2 oz. glacé cherries
1 oz. angelica
2 oz. chopped mixed peel
3 oz. butter
3 oz. caster sugar
2 egg yolks

Roll out the pastry and use to line a 7 in. fluted flan ring. Chop the cherries and angelica, or snip them with scissors, mix them with the peel and cover the base of the flan case evenly with the fruit.

Put the butter, sugar and egg yolks in a small pan over low heat, and beat steadily with a wooden spoon. Bring the mixture to the boil and pour it over the fruit. Bake the tart in the centre of the pre-heated oven, at 375°F (mark 5), for about 40 minutes.

Mince Pies

PREPARATION TIME: *35 min.*
COOKING TIME: *about 20 min.*

INGREDIENTS *(for 20–22)*:
12 oz. shortcrust pastry
1 lb. mincemeat
Milk or egg glaze (optional)
Icing sugar for dusting

Roll out the pastry, about ⅛ in. thick. Use a 3 in. fluted pastry cutter to stamp out 20–22 rounds and a 2¼ in. fluted cutter to stamp out an equal amount of rounds; re-roll the pastry as necessary. Line 2½ in. wide patty pans with the large rounds and fill to about half their depth with mincemeat. Moisten the underside edges of the smaller rounds and place them, damp side down, over the mincemeat. Press the edges of the pastry lightly together, make a small slit in the top of each pie and glaze with milk or egg white.

Set the patty pans on baking trays and bake just above the centre of a pre-heated oven, at 425°F (mark 7) for 20 minutes or until light golden brown.

Remove the mince pies from the tins with a round-bladed knife. Leave to cool on a wire rack and serve warm or cold, dusted with sifted icing sugar.

Plum and Cinnamon Pie

PREPARATION TIME: *15 min.*
COOKING TIME: *40 min.*
STANDING TIME: *1 hour*

INGREDIENTS *(for 6)*:
8 oz. American stir 'n' stir pastry
2 16 oz. tins golden plums
1 level tablespoon fine tapioca
¼ level teaspoon powdered cinnamon
1 oz. butter
1 egg white
Granulated sugar

Drain the plums, reserving the syrup, and remove the stones. Blend the tapioca and cinnamon in a bowl with 6 tablespoons of the plum syrup and leave it to stand for 30 minutes.

Roll out half the prepared pastry and use it to line a 10 in. pie plate. Mix the plums with the tapioca mixture and spoon it over the pastry base; dot with butter. Roll out the remaining pastry for the lid and cover the pie. Seal the edges, knock them up and make a slit in the lid. Brush the top with beaten egg white and dust generously with sugar. Chill for 30 minutes.

Set the pie on a heated baking tray and bake in the centre of a pre-heated oven at 400°F (mark 6) for about 40 minutes. Serve the pie warm, with whipped cream.

Rum and Butter Tarts

PREPARATION TIME: *15 min.*
COOKING TIME: *15–20 min.*

INGREDIENTS: *(for 12–14 tarts)*:
4 oz. shortcrust pastry
3 oz. currants
1 oz. butter
3½ oz. light soft brown sugar
1 tablespoon single cream or top of the milk
Rum or rum essence
½ egg or 1 egg yolk

Cover the currants with boiling water and leave them to stand until they are plump – about 10 minutes; drain thoroughly. Roll out the pastry and use to line 12–14 patty tins about 2½ in. wide. Use a plain or fluted pastry cutter.

Melt the butter in a small pan, remove from the heat and stir in the sugar, cream and rum to taste. Add the currants and stir in the thoroughly beaten egg.

Using a teaspoon, divide the currant mixture evenly between the small tarts. Do not let the filling come more than three-quarters up the pastry. Bake just above the centre of an oven pre-heated to 375°F (mark 5) for 15–20 minutes or until the pastry is crisp and the filling golden.

Cheese Straws

PREPARATION TIME: *10 min.*
COOKING TIME: *12 min.*

INGREDIENTS:
4 oz. cheese pastry

Roll out the prepared pastry as thinly as possible to a rectangle. Trim the edges evenly, then cut the pastry into strips, ¼ in. wide and 2 in. long, using a floured knife blade. Set the straws on greased baking trays and bake just above the centre of a pre-heated oven, at 400°F (mark 6), for 12 minutes, or until golden.

Leave the cheese straws to cool on a wire rack.

SUET CRUST PASTRY

This traditional British pastry is used for steamed or boiled savoury and sweet puddings, and for roly-poly puddings and dumplings. Suet is available already shredded and pre-packed, but for the best results use fresh beef suet. Correct mixing and handling achieve a pastry of a light spongy texture. For an even lighter texture replace 2 oz. of the measured flour with 2 oz. fresh white breadcrumbs.

PREPARATION TIME: *15 min.*
RESTING TIME: *15 min.*

INGREDIENTS *(for 2 pint pudding)*:
8 oz. self-raising flour or 8 oz. plain flour and 3 level teaspoons baking powder
½ level teaspoon salt
4 oz. shredded suet
¼ pint cold water (approx.)

Sift the flour and salt into a bowl (together with baking powder if plain flour is used). Add the suet – remove the skin from fresh suet, then grate or chop it finely with a little of the flour to prevent sticking – and mix thoroughly. Using a round-bladed knife, stir in the water to form a light, elastic dough. Turn the dough on to a lightly floured surface, and sprinkle it with a little flour. Knead the dough lightly with the fingertips and shape it into a ball. Put the dough on a plate and cover with an inverted bowl; leave to rest for 10–15 minutes while the filling is prepared.

Beef and Carrot Pudding

PREPARATION TIME: *20 min.*
COOKING TIME: *2 hours*

INGREDIENTS *(for 4)*:
8 oz. suet pastry
½ lb. onions
2 oz. dripping
1 lb. lean minced beef
½ lb. carrots
2 tablespoons ready-made brown sauce
1 level teaspoon mixed herbs
2 level tablespoons flour
½ pint beef stock
Salt and black pepper

Peel and finely chop the onions. Melt the dripping in a pan over moderate heat and fry the onions until they begin to colour. Stir in the minced beef and coarsely grate the peeled carrots straight into the pan. Cook for a further 5 minutes, stirring occasionally. Stir in the brown sauce, herbs, flour and the stock. Season to taste with salt and black pepper, and remove the pan from the heat. Leave the beef mixture to cool.

Line a 2 pint pudding basin with the prepared suet crust and spoon the mince mixture into the basin. Cover with the pastry lid, and seal the edges. Cover the pudding with paper and a napkin, and set the basin in a large saucepan. Pour boiling water into the pan until the water reaches halfway up the sides of the basin.

Cover the saucepan with a lid and simmer for 2 hours. Top up the pan with boiling water when necessary. Serve the pudding straight from the basin, with boiled floury potatoes.

Lining a Pudding Basin

Grease a 2 pint pudding basin. Cut one quarter from the prepared suet pastry and set it aside for the lid. Roll out the remaining pastry, on a floured surface, to a circle, 2 in. wider than the top of the basin and about ¼ in. thick. Sprinkle the pastry with flour, fold it in half and then in half again to form a triangle. Roll the pastry lightly towards the point.

Place the pastry triangle inside the basin, point downwards, and

Pastry/6

LINING AND COVERING A PUDDING BASIN

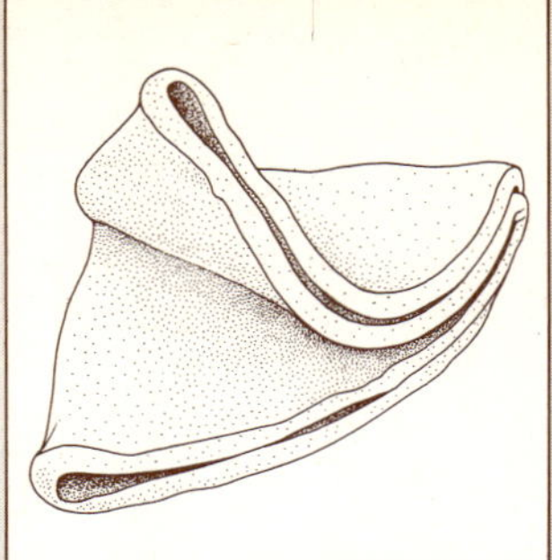

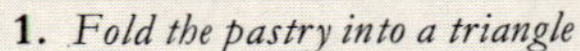

1. *Fold the pastry into a triangle*

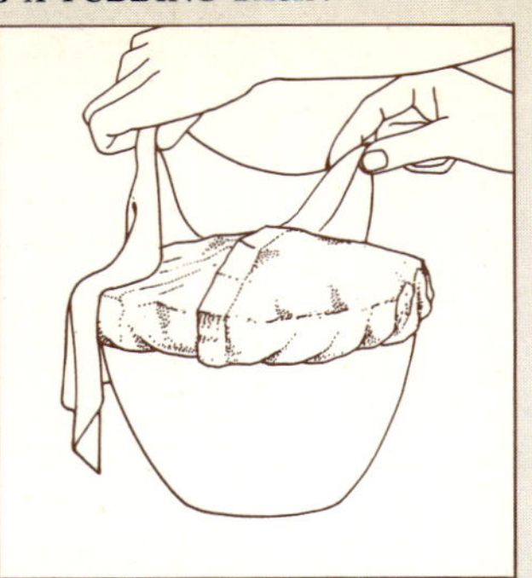

3. *Cover pudding with a cloth*

2. *Set pastry, point down, in basin*

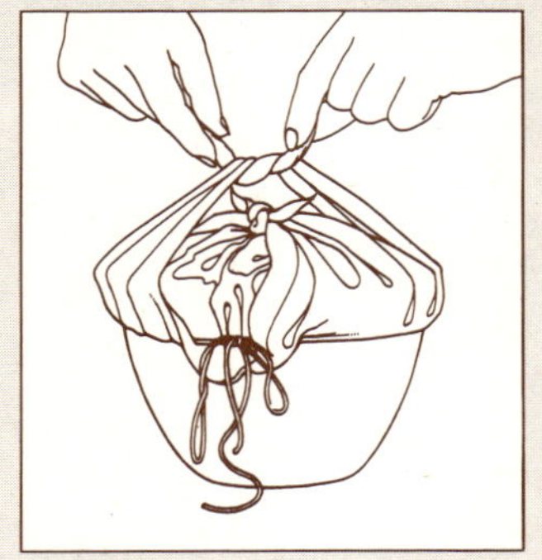

4. *Knot the ends over pudding*

unfold it, moulding it to shape. Spoon in the prepared filling. Turn the pastry overhanging the rim of the basin in over the filling and brush with water.

Roll out the remaining pastry to a circle that fits the top of the basin. Lift the pastry lid on the rolling pin and lay it over the filling. Press the edges firmly together to seal them.

Fold a pleat in a square of kitchen foil or buttered grease-proof paper – the pleat allows the pudding to rise during cooking. Place the paper over the pudding and twist it under the rim of the basin. Cover the top of the pudding with a clean napkin or cloth, tie it securely with string below the rim and tie the ends into a knot on top of the pudding.

Apple and Ginger Roll

PREPARATION TIME: *30 min.*
COOKING TIME: *$1\frac{1}{2}$ hours*

INGREDIENTS *(for 8)*:
8 oz. suet crust
1 lb. cooking apples
$\frac{1}{2}$–1 level teaspoon ground ginger
2 oz. Demerara sugar
2 oz. sultanas
Caster sugar

Put a large saucepan, half full of water, on to boil. Peel and core the apples, then cut them into even, not too thin slices and put them in a bowl. Mix the ginger and the Demerara sugar together and mix them with the apples.

Roll the prepared suet crust pastry into a rectangle about $\frac{1}{4}$ in. thick. The width of the rectangle must be at least 2 in. smaller than the diameter of the sauce-pan. Spread the apple filling over the pastry to within $\frac{1}{2}$ in. of the edges, and sprinkle with the sultanas. Turn the edges in over the filling and brush them with water. Roll up the pastry from the longest side and wrap it in kitchen foil, making a pleat in it to allow for expansion during cooking. Leave a short space at each end and twist the foil tightly to seal.

Place a heat-proof inverted plate in the pan. Lower the roll into the water and bring it back to the boil. Reduce the heat, cover the pan with a lid and boil gently for $1\frac{1}{2}$ hours. Add more boiling water, if necessary, to keep the roll covered. Lift the roll carefully from the saucepan with a fish slice. Leave it to stand for a few minutes, then remove the foil. Put the apple roll on a hot serving dish and dredge with caster sugar. Serve at once with a custard or butter-scotch sauce.

Dumplings

PREPARATION TIME: *5 min.*
COOKING TIME: *15 min.*

INGREDIENTS *(8 dumplings)*:
4 oz. suet crust pastry
Salt and black pepper
Mixed herbs or chopped parsley or 1 oz. grated cheese

Half fill a large saucepan with water and put it to boil. Make the pastry as described in the basic recipe, adding the herbs or cheese to the dry mix. Divide the pastry into eight equal pieces, and shape these into balls.

Put the dumplings into the boiling water, bring it back to the boil, then reduce heat and cover the pan. Simmer gently for 15 minutes – the dumplings will break up if the water is allowed to boil rapidly. The dumplings can be used as garnish for soups or they may be added to casserole dishes for the last 15 minutes.

HOT-WATER CRUST PASTRY

This crisp pastry has evolved from the original coffer paste. It is used for raised savoury meat and game pies and is usually served cold. The pastry is moulded by hand while still warm or fitted into a loose-bottomed cake tin or pie mould.

PREPARATION TIME: *15 min.*
RESTING TIME: *20 min.*

INGREDIENTS:
12 oz. plain flour
$\frac{1}{2}$ level teaspoon salt
4 oz. lard or soft table margarine
1 egg yolk

Sift the flour and salt into a warmed bowl. Put the fat with $\frac{1}{4}$ pint water into a small sauce-pan over low heat until the fat has melted, then bring to the boil. Make a well in the flour and drop in the egg yolk. Cover the egg with a little of the flour, then quickly add the hot fat mixture, stirring with a wooden spoon until the mixture is cool enough to handle.

Turn the dough on to a lightly floured surface and knead it quickly until soft and pliable. Shape the dough into a ball, put it on a warm plate and cover with an inverted bowl. Leave in a warm place for 20 minutes.

MOULDING AND FILLING A RAISED HOT-WATER CRUST PIE

1. *Flour a 2 lb. jam jar*

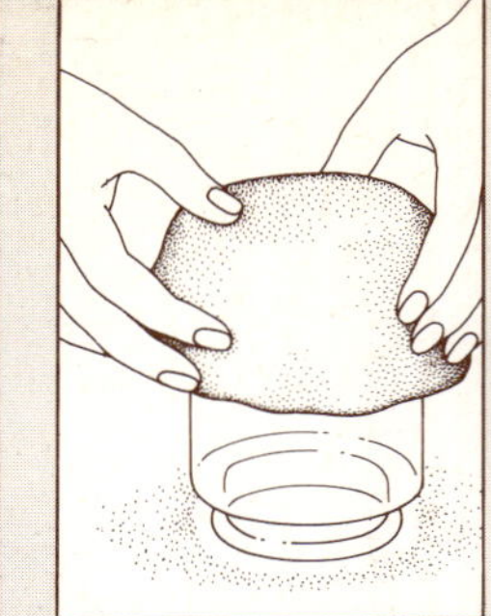
2. *Mould dough over base*

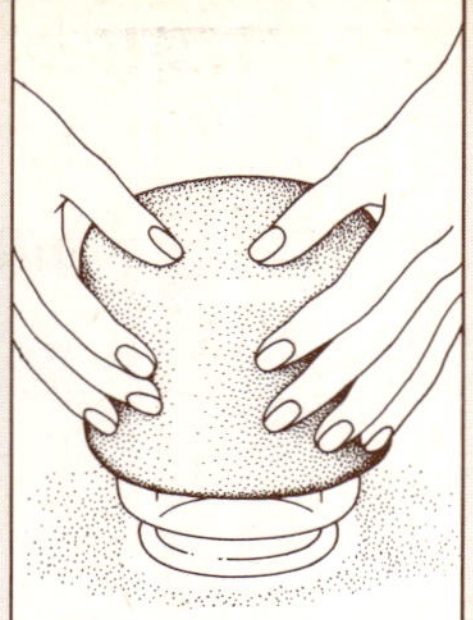
3. *Leave to cool on jar*

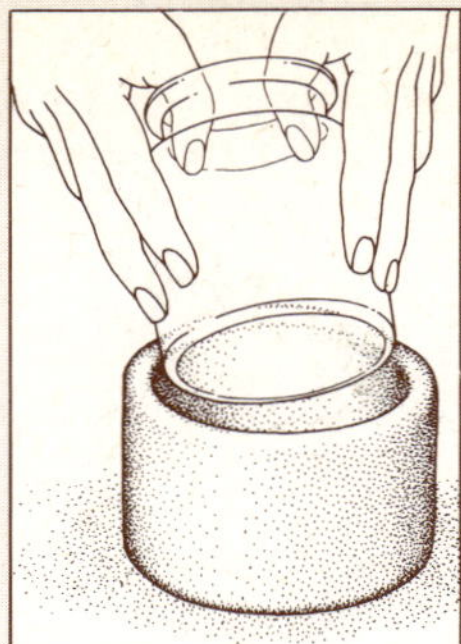
4. *Ease out the jar*

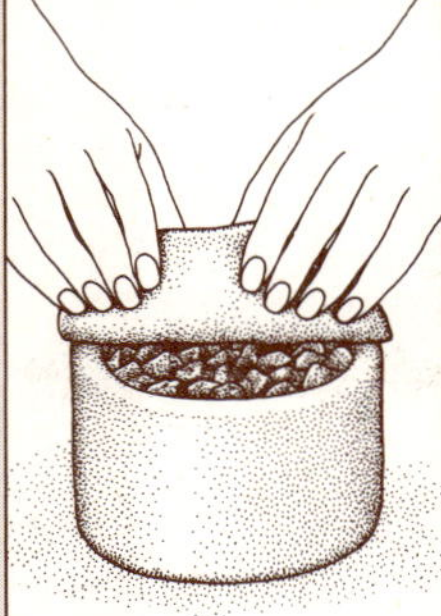
5. *Cover the filled pie*

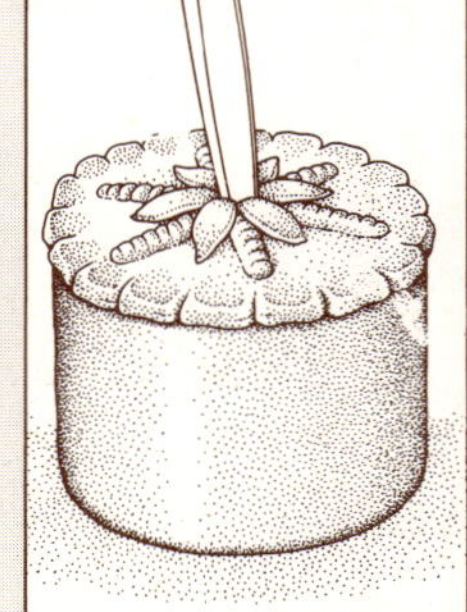
6. *Cut hole in lid*

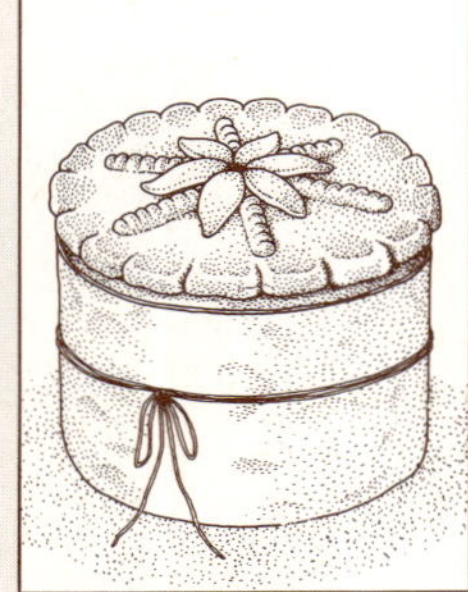
7. *Protect with paper*

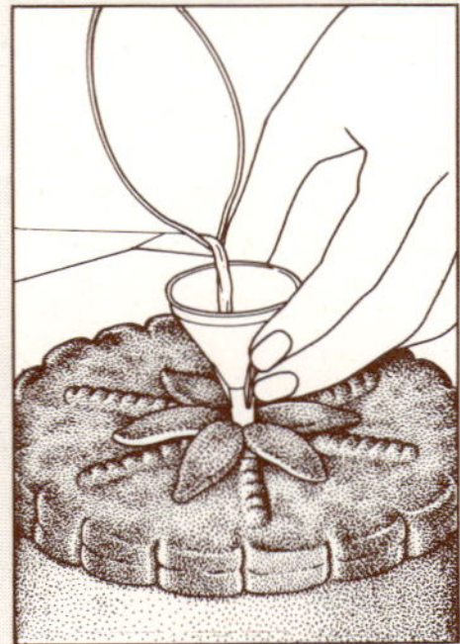
8. *Pour in liquid stock*

To mould the pastry, cut off one-third of the dough and set aside for the lid; keep it warm. Roll out the pastry thickly and use to line a hinged tin pie mould or a loose-bottomed cake tin set on a baking tray, both thoroughly greased. Alternatively, flour an empty 2 lb. jam jar, place the ball of warm dough on its base and carefully mould the dough evenly over the base and two-thirds down the sides of the jar. Set the jar aside while the dough cools and settles, then carefully ease out the jar. Spoon the filling into the pastry mould, roll out the remaining pastry for the lid, moisten the edges with water or egg glaze and cover the filling with the pastry lid. Seal the edges firmly. Cut a slit in the pastry lid and decorate the top.

Pastry moulded round a jar should have a protective band of foil tied round it to prevent the pie collapsing during baking.

Raised Veal and Bacon Pie

A raised hot-water crust pie takes time and is therefore better made in a large quantity. Cook the pie the day before to give the jellied stock time to set.

PREPARATION TIME: *1 hour*
COOKING TIME: *about 6 hours*

INGREDIENTS *(for 8)*:
PASTRY:
1 lb. plain flour
1 level teaspoon salt
1 egg yolk
6 oz. lard
JELLIED VEAL STOCK:
2 lb. veal bones, chopped
1 carrot
1 onion
2 bay leaves
6 peppercorns
FILLING:
1 lb. lean pork
¾ lb. pie veal
½ lb. lean streaky bacon
1 onion
½ level teaspoon salt
¼ level teaspoon black pepper
½ level teaspoon dried sage
Grated rind of half lemon
1 tablespoon chopped parsley
½ lb. pork sausage meat
Egg for glazing

Prepare the stock first: put the chopped veal bones with the cleaned carrot and peeled onion in a large saucepan. Add the bay leaves and peppercorns and enough water to cover. Bring to the boil, remove the scum from the surface, then cover the pan with a lid. Reduce the heat and simmer the stock for 2½ hours. Strain the stock through muslin, pour it into a clean pan and reduce to about ½ pint by fast boiling. Leave to cool.

For the filling, put the pork, veal, half the bacon (with the rind removed) and the peeled onion through the coarse blade of a mincer. Mix it thoroughly in a large bowl, then add the salt, pepper, sage, lemon rind and parsley. Moisten the mixture with 3 tablespoons of the stock.

Make the pastry as in the basic method and leave it to rest. For the pie use a greased hinged pie frame, 5¾ in. wide by 7½ in. long and 3¼ in. deep, or a 7 in. loose-bottomed cake tin lined with foil. Roll out two-thirds of the pastry into a circle large enough to line the chosen mould. Fold the pastry in half and lower it into the mould, then unfold the pastry and ease it smoothly and evenly into the base and up the sides. Press the dough well into any indentations in the pie frame.

Line the base of the pastry case with sausage meat. Spoon the minced meat mixture over the top, pressing it down lightly and keeping it slightly domed. Beat the egg with salt and brush over the pastry edge. Roll out the remaining pastry to form a lid, lift it on the rolling pin over the filling. Press the lid on to the pie edge and pinch the edges firmly together to seal. Trim the pastry.

Glaze the top of the pie by brushing with egg; roll out the pastry trimmings and cut them into leaf shapes. Arrange these in a pattern on the lid and brush with more egg. Make a wide hole in the centre of the pie lid.

Set the pie on a baking tray and bake in the centre of a pre-heated oven, at 450°F (mark 8) for 20 minutes. Reduce the heat to 325°F (mark 3), cover the pie with kitchen foil and continue baking for a further 3 hours. Leave the pie to cool in the mould until quite firm. Remove the mould or tin, and when the pie is nearly cold pour the cool liquid stock slowly through a small funnel into the pie.

Leave the pie to set completely, generally for several hours, when the stock will have set to jelly round the meat. Serve the pie cold, cut into slices or wedges.

CHOUX PASTRY

This pastry is a French speciality and is used for cream buns, chocolate eclairs and profiteroles. During cooking, the pastry should treble itself in size through the natural lift of air. The feather-light pastry surrounds a large cavity which is filled with cream.

PREPARATION TIME: *20 min.*

INGREDIENTS:
2½ oz. plain flour
2 oz. butter
Pinch of salt
¼ pint milk and water mixed (half of each)
2 beaten eggs

Sift the flour and salt on to a sheet of greaseproof paper. Put the butter and the liquid in a heavy-based pan and cook over low heat until the butter melts, then raise the heat and rapidly bring the mixture to the boil. Draw the pan off the heat and pour in all the flour. Stir quickly with a wooden spoon until the flour has been absorbed by the liquid, then beat until the dough is smooth and comes away from the sides of the pan. Do not overbeat or the fat may leak out.

Cool pastry slightly, then beat in the beaten eggs, a little at a time. The pastry should be shiny and be thick enough to hold its shape, but not stiff. If the pastry is not going to be used immediately, cover the saucepan closely with a moist sheet of greaseproof paper and with the lid to keep the dough pliable.

MAKING CHOUX PASTRY

1. *Heat butter and liquid*

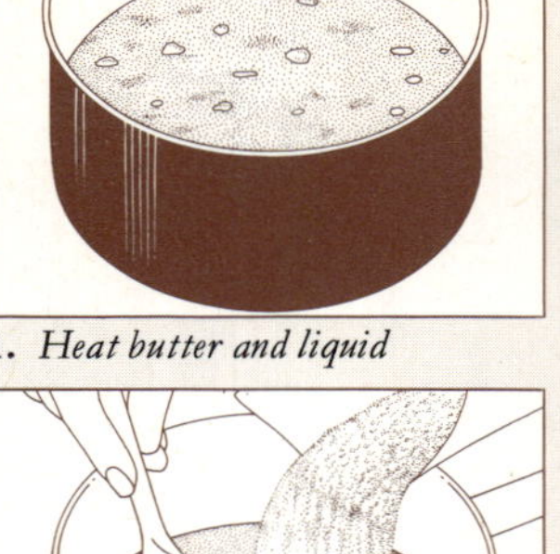

2. *Pour flour into melted butter*

3. *Beat dough until smooth*

4. *Gradually add beaten egg*

PIPING OUT CHOCOLATE ECLAIRS

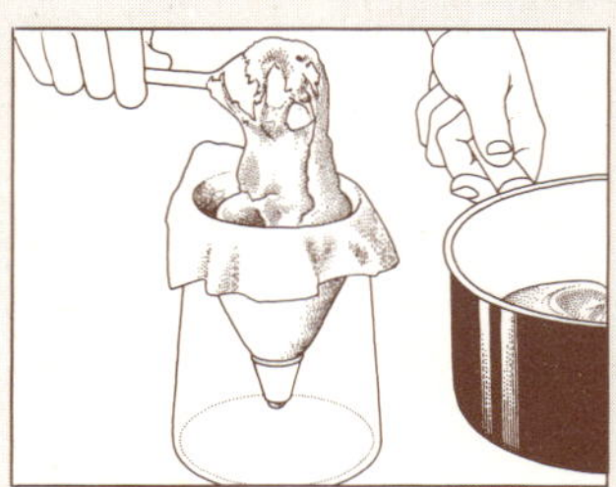

Spoon choux into a forcing bag

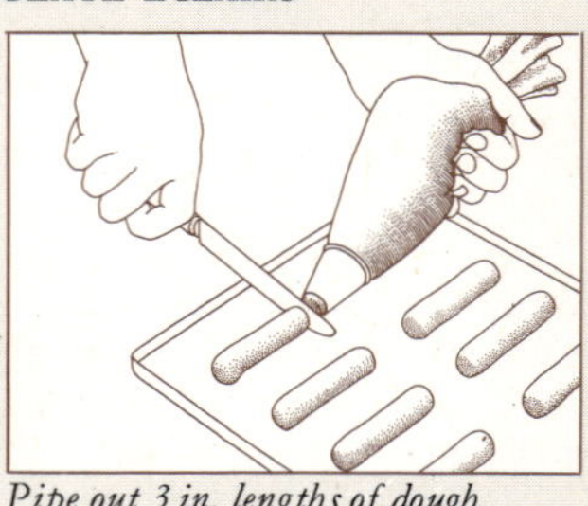

Pipe out 3 in. lengths of dough

Cheese Aigrettes

PREPARATION TIME: *20 min.*
COOKING TIME: *15–20 min.*

INGREDIENTS *(for 24)*:
1 portion choux pastry
3 oz. finely grated Cheddar cheese
Pinch of cayenne pepper
Oil or fat for deep frying

Make the pastry, following the basic recipe, and beat in the finely grated cheese and cayenne pepper after the eggs. Heat about 2½ in. of corn oil or fat in a deep fryer, without a basket, to 375°F or until a cube of bread turns golden in 60 seconds. Drop teaspoons of the pastry into the hot fat, about six at a time, and fry for 4–6 minutes until puffed and golden brown. Lift the cheese puffs out with a perforated spoon and leave to drain on absorbent kitchen paper.

Pile the cheese aigrettes on to a hot serving dish and dust with more grated cheese.

Cream Buns

PREPARATION TIME: *20 min.*
COOKING TIME: *50 min.*

INGREDIENTS *(for 10)*:
1 portion choux pastry
½ pint double cream
Icing sugar

The characteristic light, crisp texture and crazy-paving tops of these cream buns are achieved by baking the pastry in its own steam. A large, shallow tin with a tight-fitting lid is necessary, or use a heavy baking tray and invert a deep roasting tin over it. Seal the join with a flour and water paste after the choux buns have been placed inside.

Spoon the warm choux pastry into a forcing bag fitted with a ½ in. plain meringue nozzle. Pipe small rounds of the pastry on to the greased tray, setting the buns well apart. Cover the tray with the tin and bake just above the centre of an oven pre-heated to 400°F (mark 6) for 40–50 minutes.

Leave the buns undisturbed during cooking, or the steam will escape and cause the buns to collapse. The end of the cooking time can be estimated by giving the tin a gentle shake – if the buns are baked they will rattle.

Cool the buns on a wire rack, then make a slit through the base and fill them with whipped cream; dust with icing sugar.

Chocolate Eclairs

PREPARATION TIME: *20 min.*
COOKING TIME: *25–30 min.*

INGREDIENTS *(for 12–16):*
1 portion choux pastry
½ pint double cream
1 level tablespoon caster sugar
Chocolate glacé icing from ½ lb. icing sugar

Make up the choux pastry and spoon it into a forcing bag fitted with a ½ in. plain meringue nozzle. Pipe out 3 in. lengths on to a greased baking tray, starting with the end of the nozzle touching the tray and lifting it while pressing the mixture out. Cut off the required lengths with a wet knife.

Bake the eclairs just above the centre of an oven pre-heated to 425°F (mark 7) for about 20 minutes. If the eclairs are not thoroughly dry, reduce the heat to 350°F (mark 4) and continue baking for a further 10 minutes. Remove the eclairs from the oven, slit them down one side to let the steam escape and leave on a wire rack to cool. Whisk the cream and sweeten it with sugar.

When the eclairs are cold, fill them with whipped cream, using a forcing bag and plain nozzle; cover the tops with chocolate glacé icing.

Profiteroles

PREPARATION TIME: *1 hour*
COOKING TIME: *15 min.*

INGREDIENTS *(for 20–25):*
1 portion choux pastry
½ pint double or whipping cream
Icing sugar
¼ lb. plain dark chocolate
1 small tin evaporated milk

Make up the choux pastry and spoon it into a forcing bag fitted with a plain ½ in. vegetable nozzle. Pipe 20–25 small bun shapes, well apart, on to greased baking trays, and bake in a pre-heated oven, in the centre or just above, at 425°F (mark 7) for about 15 minutes until well risen, puffed and crisp. If the profiteroles are not thoroughly dry after 15 minutes, reduce the heat to 350°F (mark 4) and continue baking for a further 10 minutes. Cool on a wire rack.

Split the buns not quite in half, lengthways. Fill the hollow centres with whipped cream and dust the tops with sifted icing sugar. To serve, carefully pile the profiteroles into a pyramid on a serving dish and pour a little chocolate sauce over them; serve the remainder separately.

To make the sauce, melt the chocolate, broken into pieces, in a bowl over a pan of hot water. Stir in the evaporated milk and beat thoroughly.

FLAKED PASTRIES

These include flaky pastry, rough puff pastry and puff pastry, all of which are characterised by fat and air being trapped between thin layers of dough. During baking the trapped air expands and lifts the pastry into several flimsy and crisp layers.

Certain procedures are common to all three pastries to ensure crisp flakes: 1. Handle the pastry lightly and as little as possible; 2. The fat and the dough should have the same consistency and temperature – the fat is therefore made pliable on a plate before use; 3. To prevent the fat from melting out during baking, and thus spoiling the texture, the pastry must be chilled during and after making, and before baking; 4. Roll out the pastry evenly; do not let the rolling pin go over the edges as this will force out the air, and never stretch the pastry; 5. Before baking brush the top of the shaped pastry with beaten egg glaze, but do not let it drip down.

For lining pie dishes and flan cases, see Shortcrust pastry.

FLAKY PASTRY

This pastry is used as crusts for savoury pies, for Eccles cakes, sausage rolls, jam puffs and cream horns. It should be made in a cool atmosphere, and it is not advisable to make flaky pastry in hot weather.

PREPARATION TIME: *30 min.*
RESTING TIME: *about 2 hours*

INGREDIENTS *(for 1¼ lb.):*
8 oz. plain flour
½ level teaspoon salt
3 oz. lard
3 oz. butter or margarine
7 tablespoons iced water (approx.)
1 teaspoon lemon juice

PREPARING FLAKY PASTRY

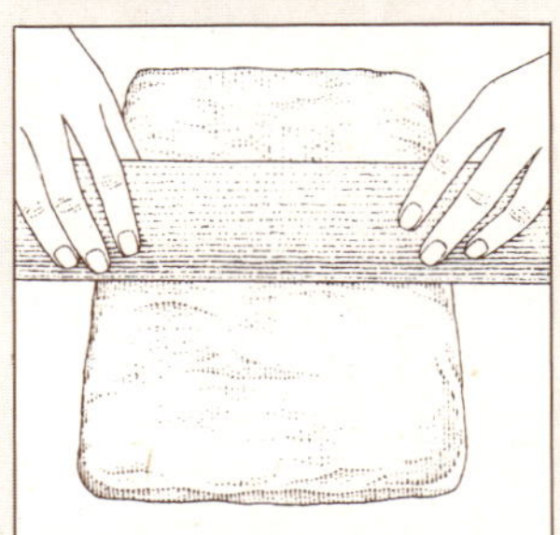
Roll out the cooled dough

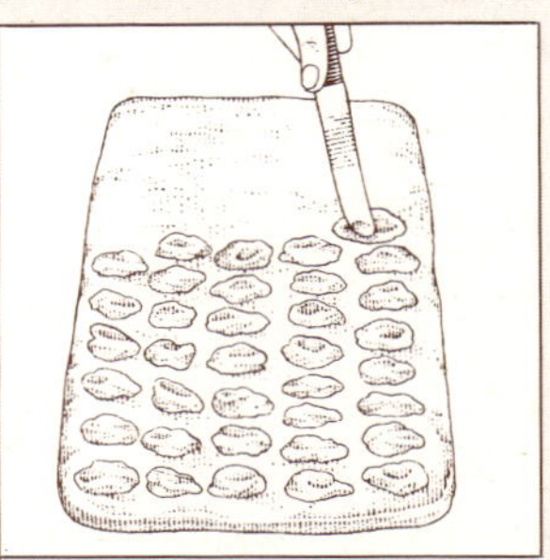
Dot fat over two-thirds of pastry

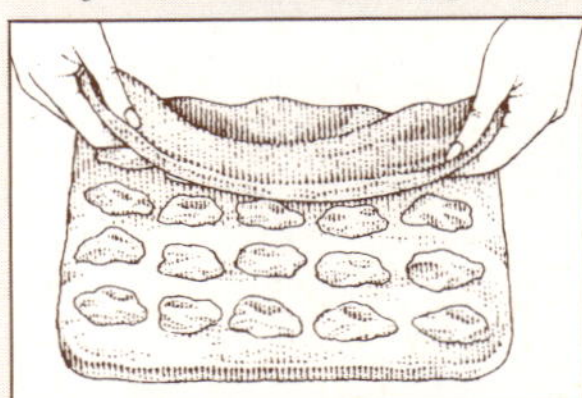
Fold unbuttered dough up

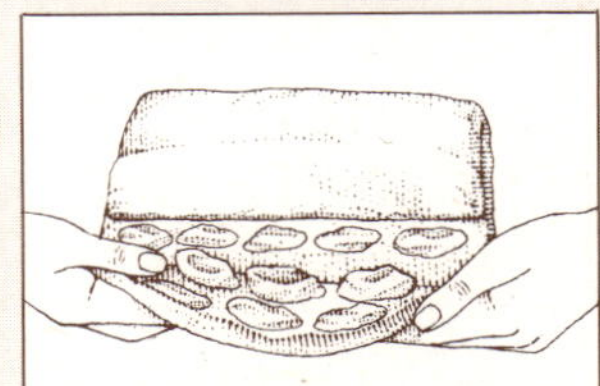
Fold buttered dough over

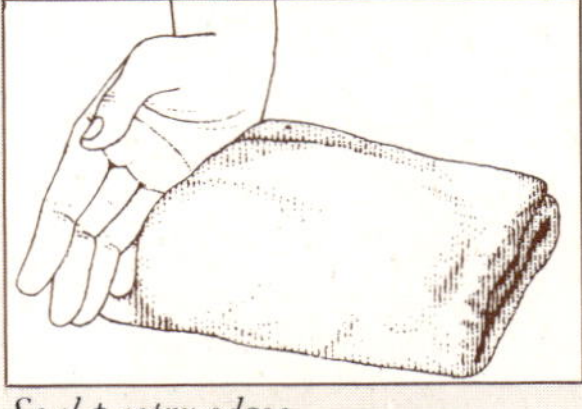
Seal pastry edges

Eccles cakes

Cream horns

Rough puff pastry

Sift the flour and salt into a wide bowl. Work the lard and butter on a plate until evenly blended, and divide it into four equal portions. Rub one portion of the fat into the flour with the fingertips until the mixture resembles breadcrumbs. Add the water and lemon juice and mix the ingredients with a round-bladed knife to a soft, manageable dough. Turn it out on to a lightly floured surface and knead until all cracks have disappeared. Cover the dough with a clean polythene bag and leave it to rest in a cool place for 20 minutes. Keep the fat cool as well.

On a lightly floured surface roll out the dough, about 24 in. long, 8 in. wide and ¼ in. thick. Brush off all surplus flour. Cut another quarter of the fat into small flakes and dot them evenly over two-thirds of the pastry and to within ½ in. of the edges. Fold the unbuttered third of the pastry over the fat and fold the buttered top third down. Turn the dough so that the folded edge points to the left and seal all the edges firmly with the side of the little finger.

Cover the pastry with a polythene bag and leave it to rest again in a cool place for about 20 minutes.

Turn the pastry so that the fold points to the right-hand side. Roll the pastry out as before, cover two-thirds with another quarter of fat, and repeat the folding, sealing and resting as before. Continue with the remaining fat, giving the pastry a half-turn between each rolling. Finally, roll out the pastry to the original rectangle, brush off any surplus flour, fold it up and wrap it loosely in polythene. Leave it to rest in a cool place for at least 30 minutes before shaping. Bake in the centre of a pre-heated oven, at 425°F (mark 7).

Eccles Cakes

PREPARATION TIME: *30 min.*
COOKING TIME: *15 min.*

INGREDIENTS *(for 10–12 cakes):*
Half portion flaky pastry
1 oz. unsalted butter
1 oz. soft brown sugar
1 oz. chopped mixed peel
2 oz. currants
1 egg white
Caster sugar

Make the filling for these little cakes first: beat the butter and sugar until pale and fluffy. Chop the peel finely and add to the creamed butter, together with the currants. Roll out the prepared pastry, ¼ in. thick. Cut it into rounds with a 3 in. plain cutter.

Put a teaspoon of the filling in the centre of each pastry round and draw the edges together to cover the filling completely. Reshape each cake into a round. Turn the cakes over and roll them lightly into flat rounds until the currants just show through the pastry. Score the top of the cakes into a lattice pattern.

Leave the cakes to rest on greased baking trays for 10 minutes in a cool place. Then brush them with lightly beaten egg white and sprinkle generously with caster sugar. Bake the cakes towards the top of the oven, pre-heated to 425°F (mark 7), for about 15 minutes or until golden and puffed.

Cream Horns

PREPARATION TIME: *30 min.*
COOKING TIME: *10 min.*

INGREDIENTS *(for 8 horns):*
Half portion flaky pastry
1 egg
Raspberry or black currant jam
5 fluid oz. double cream
4 tablespoons single cream
Icing sugar

Roll the prepared pastry out to a strip 24 in. long and 4 in. wide. Beat the egg and brush it over the pastry. Cut the pastry into eight ribbons, 24 in. long and ½ in. wide, using a sharp knife. Wind each pastry strip round a cream horn tin, starting at the tip and with the glazed side of the pastry outside; overlap each turn by about ⅛ in. As it rises during baking, the pastry should come just short of the metal rim of the horn. Set the moist horns on a baking tray, join downwards.

Bake towards the top of a pre-heated oven at 425°F (mark 7) for 8–10 minutes, until the horns are light golden. Leave to cool for a few minutes, then with one hand grip the rim of each tin with a clean cloth and carefully twist the tin. Hold the pastry lightly in the other hand and ease it off the tin. Leave the horns to cool completely, then put a teaspoon of jam into the base of each horn. Just before serving, whip the two creams and spoon them into the horns. Dust with icing sugar.

MAKING CREAM HORNS

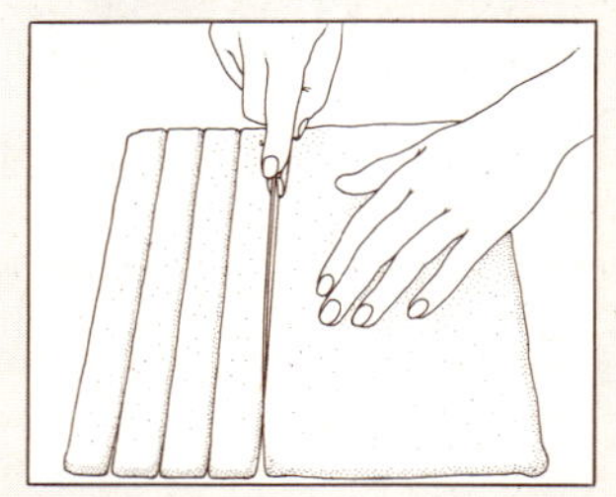

Cut pastry into ribbons

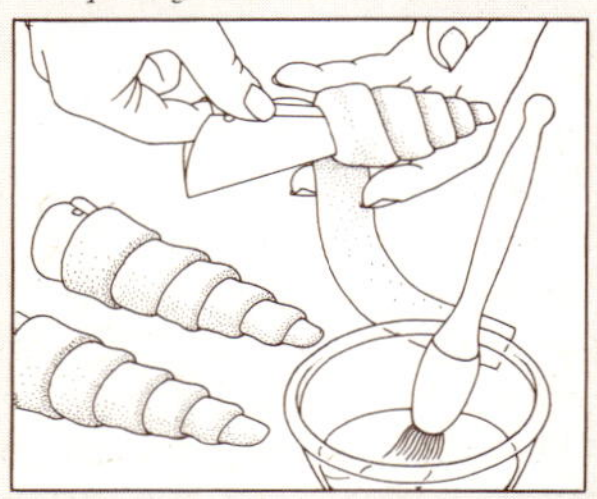

Shape pastry round tins

ROUGH PUFF PASTRY

A cross between flaky and puff pastry, rough puff pastry is easier to make than puff pastry, and is as light in texture as flaky pastry, but becomes heavy when cold. It is an excellent pastry for savoury pie crusts, sausage rolls and tarts.

PREPARATION TIME (Including resting): *1 hour*

INGREDIENTS *(for 1¼ lb.):*
6 oz. butter
8 oz. plain flour
1 level teaspoon salt
1 teaspoon lemon juice
¼ pint iced water

Cut the firm but not hard butter into walnut-sized pieces. Sift the flour and salt together into a wide bowl and add the butter, with the lemon juice and water. Mix the ingredients lightly with a round-bladed knife to form a soft elastic dough.

Turn the dough on to a floured surface and knead it lightly – as the dough is soft it needs careful handling. Shape it into a rectangle, then roll it into a strip about ¾ in. thick, 12 in. long and 4 in. wide, keeping the edges straight. The butter will be seen clearly as yellow streaks in the pastry. Fold the bottom third of the pastry up, and the upper third down. Turn the pastry so that the fold points towards the left-hand side,

MAKING ROUGH PUFF PASTRY

Add butter to sifted flour

Mix in iced water

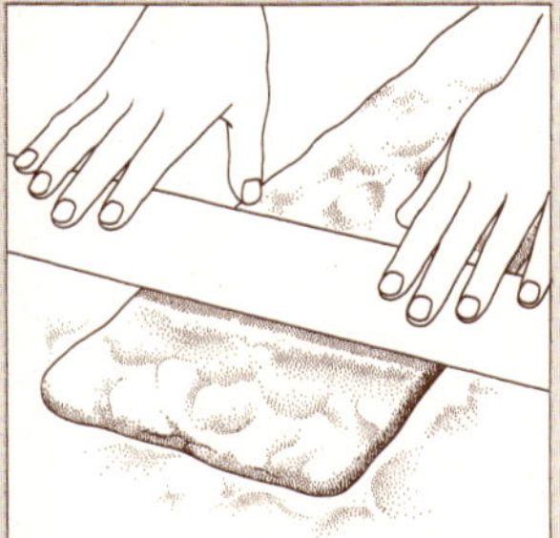

First rolling-out

Fold the dough in three

and seal the edges lightly with the edge of the little finger. Roll out the pastry again, keeping it ½ in. thick and to a rectangle of 18 in. by 6 in. Repeat the folding and rolling four times, giving the pastry a half-turn each time.

Place the pastry in a polythene bag and leave it in a cool place for 20 minutes before every two rollings. Rest the finished pastry for 10 minutes before shaping.

Bake in the centre of a pre-heated oven, at 425°F (mark 7).

SAUSAGE ROLLS

Cover sausage meat with pastry

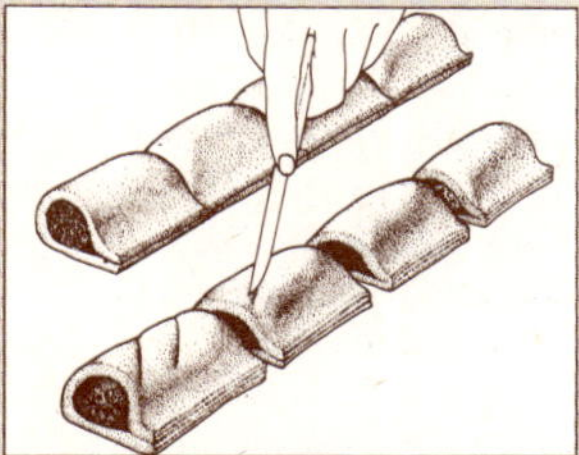

Score tops of sausage rolls

Sausage Rolls

PREPARATION TIME: *20 min.*
COOKING TIME: *30 min.*

INGREDIENTS *(for 18 rolls)*:
1 portion rough puff pastry
1 lb. sausage meat
Flour
1 egg

Cut the prepared rough puff pastry, 18 in. by 6 in., into two strips each 3 in. wide. Divide the sausage meat in half, shape it into two long rolls to fit the pastry strips, and coat the meat lightly with flour. Lay the sausage meat in the centre of the pastry strips, brush the edges with beaten egg and fold the pastry over. Seal the two long edges firmly.

Brush the two pastry lengths with beaten egg and cut them into 2 in. long pieces. Score the top of the pastry lightly with the point of a knife. Set the sausage rolls on greased baking trays and bake just above the centre of a pre-heated oven at 425°F (mark 7), for 25–30 minutes or until golden brown and puffed.

PUFF PASTRY

This is regarded as the finest and most professional pastry. It is time-consuming but well worth making if a large quantity is required. Uncooked puff pastry may also be stored in the home freezer for up to 3–4 months. When only small amounts of pastry are needed, commercially frozen and chilled puff pastry are particularly useful. Puff pastry, which is used for savoury pie crusts, as wrappings for meat and poultry, for vol-au-vents, cream horns, mille feuilles and palmiers, must be rolled out six times.

Vol-au-vents, patties and pastry crusts, which need the greatest rise and flakiness, should always be shaped from the first rolling of the finished dough. Second rolling, including trimmings from the first rolling, can be used for small items such as palmiers and crescents.

Prepared uncooked puff pastry can be stored for two to three days in the refrigerator.

PREPARATION TIME: *30–45 min.*
RESTING TIME: *2½ hours*

INGREDIENTS:
1 lb. plain flour
2 level teaspoons salt
1 lb. butter
½ pint iced water
1 teaspoon lemon juice

Sift the flour and salt into a large bowl. Cut 4 oz. of the butter into small pieces and rub it into the flour with the fingertips. Add the water and lemon juice and, using a round-bladed knife, mix the ingredients to a firm but pliable dough. Turn the dough on to a lightly floured surface and lightly knead it until smooth. Shape the pastry into a thick round and cut through half its depth in the form of a cross. Open out the four flaps and roll them out until the centre is four times as thick as the flaps. Shape the remaining firm butter to fit the centre of the dough, leaving a clear ½ in. all round. Fold the flaps over the butter, envelope style, and press the edges gently together with a rolling pin. Roll the dough into a rectangle 16 in. × 8 in., using quick short strokes. Roll lightly but firmly, back and forth, so as not to squeeze out the butter. Brush off any surplus flour between rollings. Fold the dough into three and press the edges with the edge of the little finger. Wrap the pastry in a cloth or greaseproof paper, cover with polythene and leave in a cool place for 20 minutes.

Roll out the pastry, raw edge pointed to the left, to a rectangle as before. Fold and leave to rest for 20 minutes. Repeat rolling, folding and resting four times,

Pastry/13

Vol-au-vent

Steak and wine pie

MAKING PUFF PASTRY

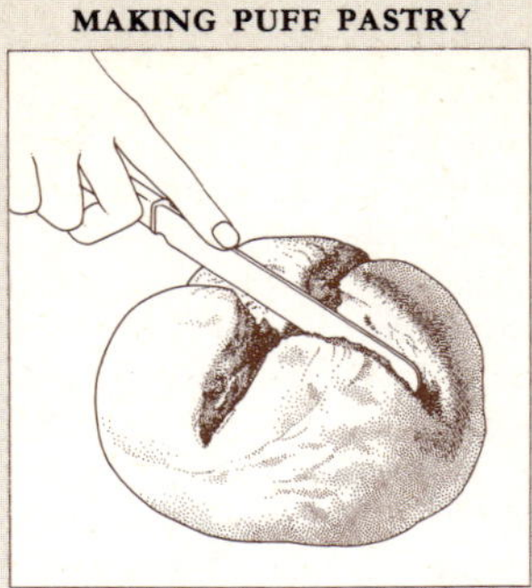

Cut a cross in rounded dough

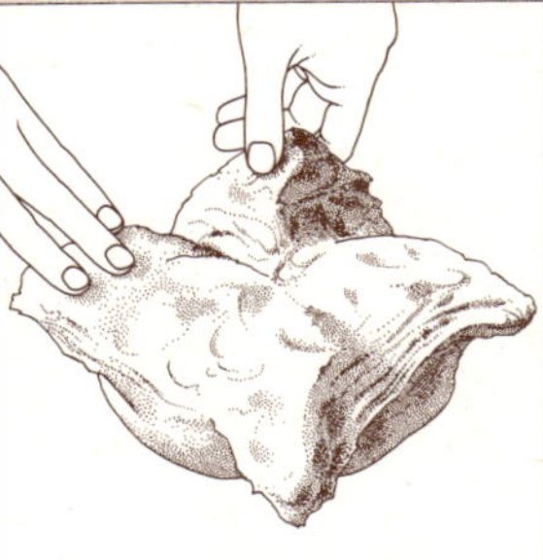

Fold out the four flaps

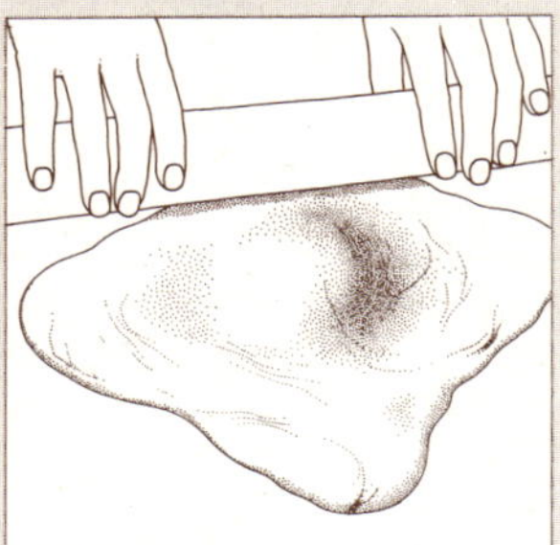

Roll out the flaps

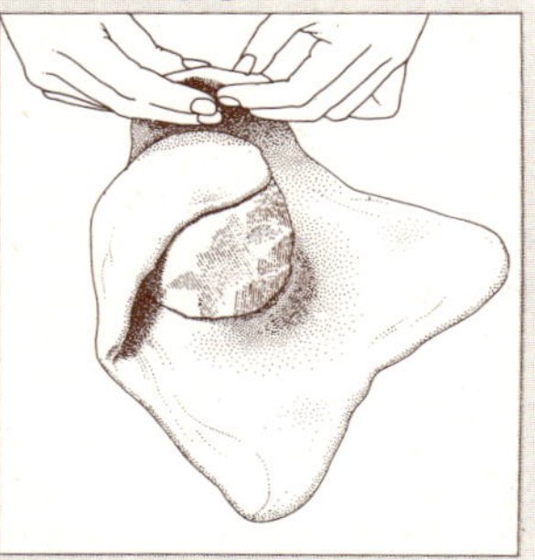

Place remaining butter in centre

giving the dough a half-turn every time. Leave the dough to rest for 30 minutes in the refrigerator before shaping it. Puff pastry, properly made, should rise about six times in height and should generally be baked in the centre, or just above, of a pre-heated oven, at 450°F (mark 8).

Vol-au-vent

The following quantity makes one large 7 in. wide vol-au-vent case, eight 3 in. cases for individual servings, or 12–14 small bouchée cases for cocktail snacks.

PREPARATION TIME: *20 min.*
COOKING TIME: *30 min.*

INGREDIENTS:
1 lb. prepared puff pastry
1 egg
6–8 oz. diced, cooked chicken, flaked salmon or 4 oz. prawns
½ pint Béchamel sauce

For a large case, roll out the pastry to a 7½ in. square. Using a 7 in. plate or lid as a guide, cut round it with a sharp knife, held at an oblique angle to give a bevelled edge. Set the pastry upside-down on a moist baking tray.

Brush the top of the pastry with beaten egg and mark a 6 in. wide circle on the pastry with a knife. Cut through half the depth of the pastry, following the mark of the inner circle. Draw a lattice pattern with the knife on the centre of the pastry triangles on the rim; rest for 15 minutes.

Bake the vol-au-vent case in the centre of a pre-heated oven at 450°F (mark 8) for about 20 minutes or until risen and brown, then reduce the heat to 350°F (mark 4) for a further 20 minutes.

When cooked, carefully ease out the pastry lid and discard any soft pastry from the centre. Fill the case with chicken, salmon or prawns blended with the Béchamel sauce.

Baked vol-au-vent case: scoop out the centre half-cooked pastry

Small vol-au-vent cases are made in a similar way. The pastry should be rolled out ½ in. thick and cut into 3 in. rounds for the cases and 1½ in. rounds for the lids. Bake in a pre-heated oven at 450°F (mark 8) for 20 minutes. For bouchée cases, roll the pastry out, ¼ in. thick, and use 2 in. and 1 in. cutters for cases and lids respectively. Bake for about 15 minutes.

Crescents Roll the trimmings out, ¼ in. thick, and cut them into narrow, 4–6 in. lengths. Shape these into crescents, set on a moist baking tray and brush with milk. Bake for barely 10 minutes, until puffed and golden, in a pre-heated oven, at 450°F (mark 8). Use as a hot garnish with fish dishes and casseroles.

Steak and Wine Pie

PREPARATION TIME: *45 min.*
COOKING TIME: *3 hours*

INGREDIENTS *(for 6)*:
12–16 oz. prepared puff pastry
2¼ lb. lean chuck steak
½ lb. kidney
1 large onion
6 oz. mushrooms
2 cloves garlic (optional)
3 oz. seasoned flour
3 tablespoons corn oil
3½ oz. butter
1 pint beef stock
½ pint dry red wine
Salt and pepper
1 egg

Trim the meat and cut it into 1 in. pieces. Skin, core and chop the kidneys. Peel and thinly slice the onion and mushrooms and peel and crush the garlic if used. Toss the meat and kidneys in seasoned flour. Heat the oil with 2 oz. of the butter in a frying pan, and fry the meat over high heat until evenly browned. Blend in the remaining seasoned flour and spoon the contents of the pan into a large casserole. Melt the remaining butter in a clean pan and fry the onion for 5 minutes; add the mushrooms and garlic and fry for 2–3 minutes. Pour in the stock and wine, bring to the boil and pour over the meat.

Cover the casserole with a lid and cook in the centre of a pre-heated oven, at 325°F (mark 3), for 1½–2 hours or until the meat is tender. Lift the meat out with a perforated spoon and put it in a 3½ pint pie dish with a pie funnel in the centre. Reduce the casserole juices by fast boiling and pour over meat. Leave to cool completely.

Roll out the pastry, ¼ in. thick, to fit the pie dish. Moisten the rim and lift the pastry over the meat. Seal the edges and brush the pastry with beaten egg. Bake in the centre of a pre-heated oven, at 450°F (mark 8), for 20 minutes until golden.

Mille Feuilles

PREPARATION TIME: *40 min.*
COOKING TIME: *20 min.*

INGREDIENTS *(for 6)*:
½ lb. prepared puff pastry
¼ lb. raspberry jam
½ pint pastry cream
6 oz. icing sugar
Cochineal

Roll out the pastry to a rectangle 10 in. by 9 in. Prick it all over with a fork. Lift the pastry on to a moist baking tray and bake just above centre of a pre-heated oven at 450°F (mark 8) for 20 minutes or until well risen and golden brown. Cool the pastry on a wire rack, then cut it in half lengthways. Spread the top of one piece with two-thirds of the raspberry jam; cover with pastry cream.

Blend the sifted icing sugar in a bowl with just enough cold water to give a coating consistency. Mix 1 tablespoon of the icing in a cup with a few drops of cochineal colouring.

Spread the remaining raspberry jam over the second piece of pastry and turn it upside-down on to the pastry cream. Press the pastries together, then cover the top of the pastry with white icing. Pipe thin lines of pink icing at ½ in. intervals, lengthways, over the white icing. Draw the tip of a knife quickly across the width of the pastry, at ½ in. intervals to give the icing a feathered effect. Leave the mille feuille to set, then cut it into six equal slices.

PÂTÉ SUCRÉE

This pastry is the French equivalent of British enriched shortcrust pastry. It is thin and crisp, yet melting in texture, and neither shrinks nor spreads during baking. Pâté sucrée is usually baked blind, but flan cases and moulds need not be weighed down.

PREPARATION TIME: *15 min.*
RESTING TIME: *1 hour*

INGREDIENTS:
4 oz. plain flour
Pinch salt
2 oz. caster sugar
2 oz. butter
2 egg yolks

Sift together the flour and salt on to a cool working surface or, preferably, a marble slab. Make a well in the centre of the flour and put in the sugar, soft butter and the egg yolks. Using the fingertips of one hand, pinch and work the sugar, butter and egg yolks together until well blended. Gradually work in all the flour from the sides and knead the pastry lightly until smooth. Leave the pastry in a cool place for at least 1 hour to rest before rolling it out. Bake in the centre of a pre-heated oven, at 350–400°F (mark 4–6).

Bateaux Saint André

PREPARATION TIME: *20 min.*
COOKING TIME: *20 min.*

INGREDIENTS *(for 6)*:
One-third portion pâté sucrée
½ lb. cooking apples
1 oz. caster sugar
½ egg white
4 oz. icing sugar

Peel, core and dice the apples and cook them with the sugar and 1 tablespoon water until they have reduced to a thick purée. Set aside to cool.

Roll out the pâté sucrée thinly and use to line six boat-shaped moulds, 4½ in. long. Proceed as described for Bateaux de Miel. Divide the apple purée equally between the pastry-lined moulds.

Whisk the egg white lightly in a small bowl, then gradually beat in the sifted icing sugar, using a wooden spoon. Spread a thin layer of this meringue mixture over each boat. Roll out the pastry trimmings thinly, cut them into short narrow strips and lay two strips across each boat.

Bake the pastry boats in the centre of a pre-heated oven, at 375°F (mark 5), for about 10 minutes, until the pastry has set and the meringue is pale beige. Leave the pastries to cool slightly, then ease the moulds away.

COMMON FAULTS IN PASTRY MAKING

Shortcrust

Hard and/or tough pastry: due to too much liquid, too little fat, over-handling or insufficient rubbing in.
Soft and crumbly pastry: too little water: too much fat, or self-raising flour used instead of plain.
Shrunk pastry: excess stretching during rolling out.
Soggy pastry: filling too moist or sugar in a sweet pie in contact with pastry. For a double crust pie, use ideally a metal pie plate and either brush pastry base with egg white or butter the pie plate before lining with pastry.

Toss the prepared fruit filling with a mixture of 1 tablespoon flour and 4 oz. caster sugar before covering with a pastry lid.
Sunken pie: oven temperature too low; cold pastry put over hot filling; too much liquid in filling, or too little filling.
Speckled pastry: undissolved sugar grains in enriched pastry crust.

Hot-water Crust

Cracked pastry: insufficient liquid; too little kneading; liquid not boiling when added to flour.
Dry, difficult-to-mould pastry: liquid not boiling when added to flour; too much liquid; dough not cooled enough to set to required shape.
Hard pastry: insufficient fat or liquid.

Suet Pastry

Heavy pastry: insufficient baking powder; water not kept on the boil during cooking.
Tough pastry: dough handled too much and rolled out excessively.
Soggy pastry: paper and cloth covering over filled pie too loose, and water not kept boiling during cooking.

Choux Pastry

Mixture too soft: insufficient cooling of the flour before adding eggs; eggs added too quickly.
Pastry did not rise: self-raising flour used; oven too cold; too short baking time.
Sinking after removal from oven: insufficient baking; further period of baking sometimes remedies this defect.

Flaky, Rough Puff and Puff Pastries

Too few layers: insufficient resting and chilling; heavy rolling causing fat to break through and intermingle with the pastry; fat too soft.
Fat running out during baking: oven too cool.
Hard and tough pastry: too much water; over-kneading.
Shrinking pastry: insufficient resting; over-stretching during rolling.

Bread/1

Ingredients

Making the dough

Home-baked bread has a strikingly different taste and texture from commercially baked loaves. Our daily bread is composed of such basic ingredients as flour, yeast, salt and liquid; enriched dough mixtures for buns and tea breads also include butter and spices, dried fruits and nuts.

In the North of England and in Scotland, where home-baking is much more popular than in the south, there are more types of flour to choose from. Flour is the most important factor in bread-making, and the so-called 'strong' flours are essential for well-made loaves. A 'strong' flour has a high gluten content (from which protein is formed) of 10–15 per cent and aids rising in combination with yeast; it absorbs liquids easily and produces bread of light and open texture.

In the south, most health shops stock strong flours, specially recommended for bread-making.

Flour

Brown flour produces a yeast dough of closer texture and with less rise than a white dough. It does not store well and should be bought as required. Wholemeal flour contains 100 per cent wheat, and wheatmeal flour has 80–90 per cent wheat including all the germ and some bran. Both these types of flour give the characteristic mealy taste to bread.

Yeast

Fresh or dried yeast may be used in bread-making. Many small private bakers will supply fresh yeast, and some supermarkets and health stores also stock it. Dried yeast is more concentrated than fresh yeast: ½ oz. or 4 level teaspoons of dried yeast is the equivalent of 1 oz. of fresh yeast.

Fresh yeast should have a creamy-beige colour, and a firm consistency which crumbles easily when broken up. It can be stored in a loosely tied polythene bag in a cool place for up to 5 days, in a refrigerator for up to a month, or in the home freezer for up to a year.

Fresh yeast is added to flour in three different ways: it is rubbed in, blended with liquid or added as a batter. Rubbing in is suitable for soft doughs, quick-breads and sweet doughs. Blending with liquid is the basic way and is suitable for all bread recipes. The batter method is best suited for rich yeast doughs, and works equally well with fresh and dried yeast. It is not advisable to cream fresh yeast with sugar, as this results in the breakdown of some of the living yeast cells.

Rubbing-in method Crumble the yeast into the sifted flour and salt with the tips of the fingers. Add the specified amount of liquid to the flour and yeast mixture to make a soft dough. Work the dough with the finger-tips to distribute the yeast evenly.

Blending with liquid Blend the yeast with part of the measured liquid; add this mixture to the flour and salt, together with the remaining liquid.

Batter method Mix one-third of the measured flour with the yeast, blended with all the liquid and 1 level teaspoon of sugar. Leave in a warm place until frothy, about 20 minutes, then add the rest of the flour, the salt and any other ingredients specified.

Dried yeast This can be stored in a tightly lidded container for up to 6 months. Dried yeast is reconstituted in some warm water (110°F). (This water should be taken from the amount to be used in the recipe, first dissolved in the proportion of 1 level teaspoon sugar to ½ pint water.) Sprinkle the yeast over the water and leave in a warm place until frothy – after about 15 minutes.

Salt

Apart from improving the flavour of bread, salt also affects the gluten in the flour. If salt is omitted, the dough rises too quickly. If there is too much salt, this kills the yeast and gives the bread a heavy or uneven texture. Measure the salt carefully.

Liquid

This may be milk, water or a mixture of both. The amount varies from recipe to recipe, depending on the absorbency of the flour. Milk adds food value and strengthens doughs, improves the keeping quality and the colour of the crust. For plain bread, however, water alone gives a better texture.

Fat

This is used in enriched yeast doughs for buns, croissants and tea breads which have a soft outer crust. Fat makes a dough soft and also slows down yeast action so that the dough rises less than plain bread dough.

Sugar

Too much sugar added to a dough mixture delays fermentation of the yeast cells; always follow the given quantities.

Making the dough

Sift the flour and the salt into a mixing bowl, make a well in the centre and add all the liquid at once. Mix it in with one hand until thoroughly incorporated. Add more flour if necessary, and beat the dough against the sides of the bowl until it comes away cleanly. Knead the dough on a lightly floured surface.

Kneading is most important, as it strengthens and develops the dough and enables it to rise. Gather the dough into a ball with the tips of the fingers, then fold the dough towards the body. Press down on the dough and away from the body with the palm of the hand. Give the dough a quarter-turn and repeat the kneading.

Knead the dough for about 10 minutes until it feels firm and elastic and no longer sticks to the

MAKING BREAD DOUGH

Pour the liquid into the flour

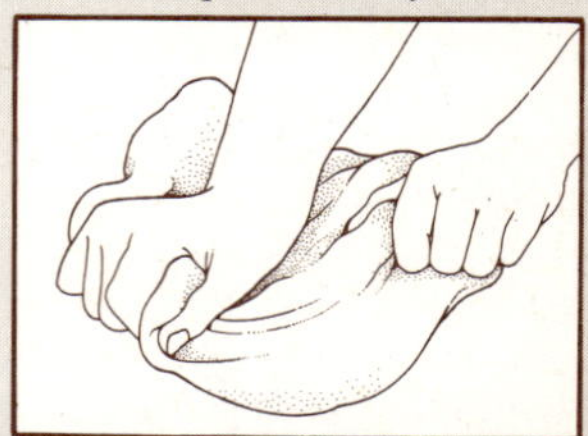

Knead until the dough is elastic

Rise dough in polythene bag

fingers – it is better to knead the dough too much rather than too little. Bread dough may be kneaded in an electric mixer.

Rising

After kneading, the dough must be set aside for rising and proving (second rising) until it has doubled in size. A large polythene bag is useful for the rising process. Pour a few drops of corn oil into the bag and swirl it round to distribute it evenly in a thin film. Put the dough in the bag, tie it loosely and leave the dough until it has doubled in size and springs back when lightly pressed with a finger. The time the dough takes to rise depends on the temperature and the surroundings, but ideally the dough should be allowed to rise slowly, at a low temperature over a long period. Allow 12 hours in a cool room or larder, and about 2 hours at normal room temperature, away from draughts. Dough left to rise in a refrigerator will need 24 hours.

If time is short, the dough can be made to rise in 45–60 minutes in a warm place, for example over a pan of warm water. Too much heat, however, may kill the yeast.

Knocking back and proving

After the initial rising the dough has to be kneaded again, to knock out the air bubbles and to ensure a good rise and even texture. Shape the kneaded dough as required and put it into tins or on to baking trays. Slip the tins or trays into oiled polythene bags and leave the loaves to rise at room temperature until double their size. This second rising is also known as proving.

Baking

Remove the tins or baking trays from the polythene bags and bake at 400–450°F (mark 6–8), according to the individual recipes. A bowl of hot water placed in the bottom of the oven creates steam, which improves the bread texture.

Storing

Place the baked and cooled loaves in clean polythene bags, leaving the end open. To refresh a crusty loaf, wrap it in kitchen foil and put in the oven at 450°F (mark 8) for about 10 minutes. Leave it to cool in the foil.

PREPARING LOAVES FOR BAKING

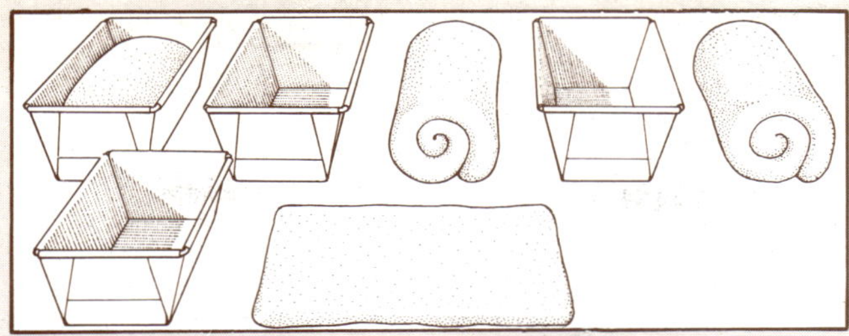

Shape or roll up risen and proven dough to fit greased loaf tins

TRADITIONAL BREAD SHAPES

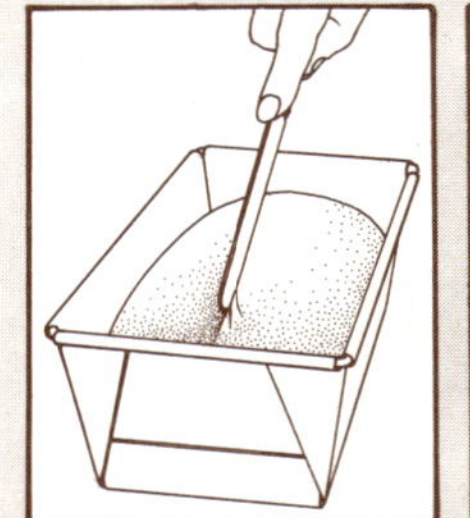

Score the top of a tin loaf with a knife

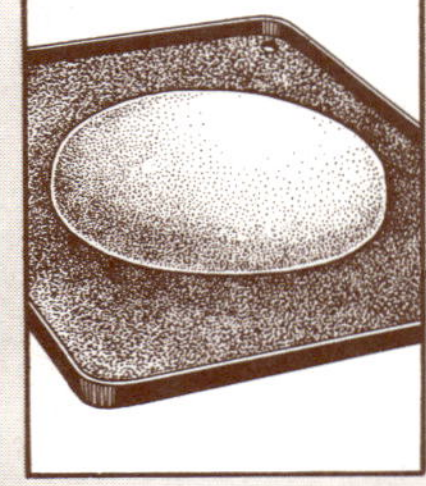

Cob loaf is a slightly flattened ball of dough

Arrange dough in a round tin for a crown loaf

White Bread

PREPARATION TIME: *25 min. (plus rising and proving)*
COOKING TIME: *30–40 min.*

INGREDIENTS *(for 4 loaves)*:
3 lb. strong plain flour
3–4 level teaspoons salt
1 oz. lard
1 oz. fresh yeast
$1\frac{1}{2}$ pints water less 3 tablespoons

Sift the flour and salt together into a large bowl and rub in the lard with the fingertips. In a small bowl, blend the yeast with $\frac{1}{2}$ pint of the measured water. Make a well in the centre of the flour and pour in the yeast liquid and the remaining water. Work the dough mixture with one hand until it leaves the sides of the bowl clean. If necessary add a little extra flour.

Turn the dough on to a lightly floured surface and knead it for about 10 minutes until smooth and elastic. Shape it into a round, then set it aside to rise until it has doubled its size.

Divide the risen dough into four equal portions on a lightly floured board. Flatten each piece firmly with the knuckles to knock out any air bubbles, then knead for 2–3 minutes. Stretch each piece of dough into an oblong the same length as the tin, ease it into the greased tin and score the dough lightly along the top. Alternatively, fold the dough into three along the long edges or roll it up like a Swiss roll. Tuck the ends under so that the dough, seam downwards, fits a 1 lb. tin.

Brush the top of the dough with lightly salted water. Place the tins in lightly oiled polythene bags and leave in a warm place to rise (prove), until the dough reaches the top of the tins. Remove the polythene, brush the top of the dough with salted water again and set the tins on baking trays.

Bake the loaves in the centre of a pre-heated oven at 450°F (mark 8) for about 30 minutes, or until the loaves shrink slightly from the sides of the tins and the upper crust is a deep golden brown. For really crusty bread, turn the loaves out of the tins on to a baking tray and return them to the oven for a further 5–10 minutes. When done, baked loaves sound hollow when tapped on the base. Leave the bread to cool on a wire rack.

Cob Loaf Roll each piece of dough into a ball, flatten it and place on a floured baking tray.

Crown Loaf Divide a quarter of the risen dough into five or six balls. Set these in a greased, 5 in. wide cake tin or a deep sandwich tin.

Bread/3

Wholemeal bread

Quick wheatmeal loaves

Enriched white bread

Wholemeal Bread

PREPARATION TIME: *20 min. (plus rising and proving)*
COOKING TIME: *30–40 min.*

INGREDIENTS *(for two 2 lb. or four 1 lb. loaves)*:
3 lb. plain wholemeal flour
1 level tablespoon caster sugar
3-4 level teaspoons salt
1 oz. lard
2 oz. fresh yeast
1½ pints warm water

Sift the flour, sugar and salt into a large bowl. Cut up the lard and rub it into the flour with the fingertips until the mixture resembles fine breadcrumbs. Blend the yeast, in a small bowl, with ½ pint of the measured water and pour it into a well in the centre of the flour; add the remaining water. Using one hand, work the mixture together and beat it until the dough leaves the bowl clean. Knead the dough on a lightly floured surface for 10 minutes.

Shape the dough into a large ball and leave it to rise in a lightly oiled polythene bag until it has doubled in size. Turn the dough on to a lightly floured surface and knead again until firm. Divide the dough into two or four equal pieces and flatten each piece firmly with the knuckles to knock out any air bubbles. Stretch and roll each piece of dough into an oblong the same length as the tin; fold it into three or roll it up like a Swiss roll. Lift the dough into the greased tins, brush the top with lightly salted water and place each tin inside an oiled polythene bag. Tie the bag loosely and leave to rise until the dough reaches the top of the tins.

Remove the tins from the bags, set them on baking trays and bake in the centre of a pre-heated oven at 450°F (mark 8) for about 30 minutes or until the loaves shrink from the sides of the tins. Cool the loaves on a wire rack and test by tapping them.

For a fancy wholemeal loaf divide a quarter of the dough into four equal pieces; shape them into rolls the width of a greased 1 lb. loaf tin and fit them, side by side, into the tin. Finish as before. For a cob loaf, shape each quarter portion of dough into a round, flatten them slightly then dust with flour and place on a floured baking tray.

Quick Wheatmeal Loaves

PREPARATION TIME: *20 min. (plus rising)*
COOKING TIME: *30–40 min.*

INGREDIENTS *(for one 1 lb. loaf and 8 rolls, or two 1 lb. loaves)*:
½ lb. plain brown flour
½ lb. strong plain white flour
2 level teaspoons salt
2 level teaspoons caster sugar
¼ oz. lard
½ oz. fresh yeast
½ pint warm water
2–3 tablespoons cracked wheat or crushed cornflakes

Sift the two flours, the salt and sugar into a bowl. Cut up the lard and rub it into the flour with the fingertips. Blend the yeast with all the warm water until the yeast has dissolved. Make a well in the centre of the flour and pour in the yeast liquid. Mix to a soft, scone-like dough, beating until it leaves the side of the bowl clean (if necessary, add a little more flour).

Divide the dough into two equal portions. Shape each piece to half fill a greased 1 lb. loaf tin and brush the top of the dough with lightly salted water; sprinkle with cracked wheat or crushed cornflakes. Place the tins on a baking tray in a lightly oiled polythene bag, tie loosely and leave in a warm place until the dough has doubled in size. Remove the polythene and bake the loaves in the centre of a pre-heated oven at 450°F (mark 8) for about 40 minutes. Test by tapping the loaves; if they sound hollow, they are baked. Cool on a wire rack.

Rolls Divide the whole, risen dough after re-kneading into 8 equal pieces. Roll each into a round on an unfloured surface, using the palm of one hand. Shake a little flour on to the palm of the hand, and press the dough down, hard at first, easing up until the rounds have the shape of a roll. Set the rolls well apart on floured baking trays, put them into oiled polythene bags and leave in a warm place until doubled.

Remove the polythene and bake the rolls just above the centre of the oven, pre-heated to 450°F (mark 8), for about 40 minutes. Cool on a wire rack.

For soft rolls, set the shaped rolls ¾ in. apart on the baking trays and sprinkle generously with flour. The rolls will bake into contact with each other along the sides and the flour on top will give a soft surface.

Flowerpot Loaves Wheatmeal bread may also be baked in flowerpots. Use clay pots – never plastic – grease them thoroughly inside and bake them empty in a hot oven several times to seal the inner surface and prevent the dough sticking. A clay flowerpot 4–5 in. wide will hold half a portion of wheatmeal dough. Finish and bake the loaf as already described.

Enriched White Bread

PREPARATION TIME: *35 min. (plus rising and proving)*
COOKING TIME: *35–45 min.*

INGREDIENTS:
1 lb. strong plain flour
1 level teaspoon caster sugar
2 level teaspoons dried yeast
8 fluid oz. warm milk
1 level teaspoon salt
2 oz. margarine
1 egg

GLAZE:
1 egg
1 level teaspoon caster sugar
1 tablespoon water
Poppy seeds (optional)

Mix 5 oz. flour, the sugar, yeast and all the milk in a large bowl: set it aside in a warm place for about 20 minutes or until frothy. Sift the remaining flour and the salt into another bowl and rub in the margarine. Make a well in the centre, add the beaten egg and the frothy yeast mixture. Mix with one hand to make a fairly soft dough that leaves the side of the bowl clean.

Turn the dough out on to a lightly floured surface, knead it for about 10 minutes until smooth, then place it in an oiled polythene bag and leave to rise and double in size. Knead the risen dough lightly on a floured surface before shaping it.

Poppy-seed Plaits Divide the dough into three, and roll each into a 12 in. long strand. Set the three strands side by side on a flat surface, and pass the left strand over the centre strand, then the right strand over the centre strand. Continue like this until the whole length is plaited. Finally join the short ends neatly together and tuck them under.

Place the plaits on a lightly greased baking tray. Beat the egg

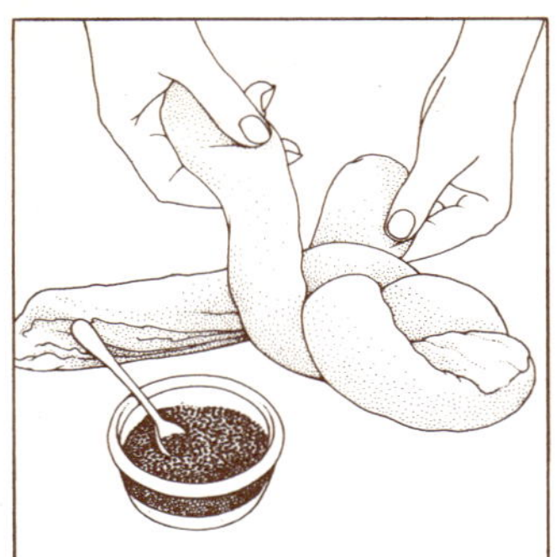

Plaited loaf: for a three-strand plait, begin crossing the dough near the top

with the sugar and water to make the glaze. Brush the plaits evenly and sprinkle with poppy seeds. Put the plaits on the tray inside a lightly oiled polythene bag and set aside to rise (prove) again until the dough has doubled in size. Remove the polythene bag and bake the loaves in the centre of a pre-heated oven at 375°F (mark 5) for 35–40 minutes. Tap the bottom of the loaves with the knuckles – if they sound hollow they are done. Cool on a wire rack.

Crown Loaf Divide all the risen dough into 12 equal pieces – about 2 oz. each. Shape these with the palm of the hand, and put them in a greased, 9 in. wide sandwich tin and place the balls in a circle around the inner edge of the tin, with three or four balls in the centre. Brush with glaze, leave to rise (prove) and bake as already described, for 45–60 minutes.

Fancy Rolls Enriched white dough is ideal for light, dinner-type rolls which can be shaped in a variety of ways. Use about 2 oz. of risen dough for each roll. Roll a piece of dough out, about 4 in. long, cut it in half lengthways and, holding each strip at both ends, twist it three times. Alternatively, roll each strip into a strand and tie it into a knot in the centre.

Shape 2 oz. pieces of dough into oblong miniature loaves and score the surface with five or six marks, at even intervals. With a scissor-point, make triangular cuts between the score marks, through the dough, so that the points are slightly raised.

Divide a 2 oz. piece of dough into three, shape into balls and set them on a baking tray in such a way that all three balls touch each other.

Alternatively, roll a 2 in. piece of dough into a thick strand and shape into a snail or 'S' form.

Brush the rolls with egg glaze and set them aside to rise (prove) until doubled in size. Bake the rolls just above the centre of a pre-heated oven, at 375°F (mark 5), for 10–15 minutes or until golden.

FANCY ROLLS

Twisting strips of dough

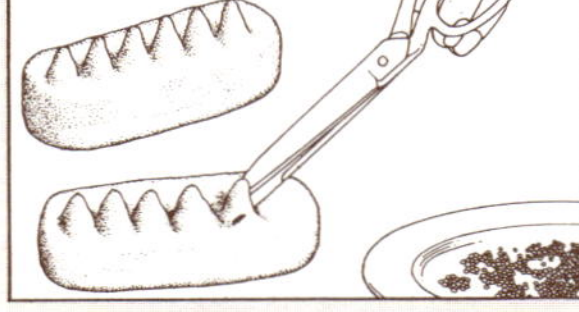

Snipping small cuts in rolls

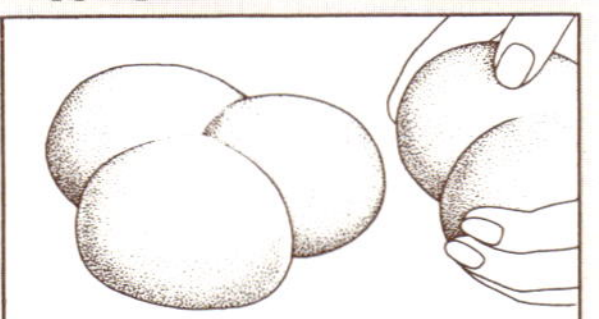

Shaping triangular rolls

Apricot and Walnut Loaf

PREPARATION TIME: *30 min. (plus rising)*
COOKING TIME: *40–45 min.*

INGREDIENTS *(for one 1 lb. loaf)*:
Half portion quick wheatmeal dough
4 oz. dried apricots
1 oz. caster sugar
2 oz. chopped walnuts
TOPPING:
1 oz. butter or firm margarine
1 oz. caster sugar
1½ oz. plain flour

Cut the dried apricots roughly with scissors and put them in a bowl or on a floured board, with the risen dough, the sugar and walnuts. Work the mixture together until no streaks can be seen. Line the bottom of a 1 lb. loaf tin with buttered greaseproof paper and grease the sides of the tin. Put the dough in the tin and set in a lightly oiled polythene bag; leave in a warm place for about 1 hour or until the dough has risen to within ½ in. of the rim of the tin.

Meanwhile, make the topping. Rub together the butter, sugar and flour in a small bowl until the mixture resembles coarse breadcrumbs. Cover the risen dough evenly with the crumb mixture, and set the tin on a baking tray. Bake in the centre of a pre-heated oven at 400°F (mark 6) for 40–45 minutes. Leave the baked loaf in the tin for 10 minutes, then turn it out to cool on a wire rack.

Sally Lunn

PREPARATION TIME: *25 min. (plus rising)*
COOKING TIME: *15–20 min.*

INGREDIENTS *(for 2 loaves)*:
1 lb. strong plain flour
2 oz. butter
¼ pint milk plus 4 tablespoons
1 level teaspoon caster sugar
½ oz. fresh yeast
2 eggs
1 level teaspoon salt
SUGAR TOPPING:
1 level tablespoon caster sugar
1 tablespoon water

Melt the butter in a small pan, then add the milk and sugar. Put the yeast in a bowl, beat the eggs and add them, with the warm milk mixture, to the yeast: blend thoroughly until the yeast has dissolved. Sift the flour and salt into a large bowl, make a well in the centre and pour in the milk mixture. Gradually incorporate the flour with the fingers of one hand and beat the dough against the bowl until it leaves the sides clean. Knead on a lightly floured surface until smooth.

Divide the dough into two equal portions, knead each piece into a ball and place it in a greased 5 in. round cake tin. Slide each tin into an oiled polythene bag and leave in a warm place for about 1 hour or until the dough has risen almost to the top of the tins.

Remove the polythene and set the tins on baking trays and bake just above the centre of a pre-heated oven at 450°F (mark 8) for 15–20 minutes. Meanwhile, make the sugar topping by heating the sugar and water in a small pan over low heat until the sugar has dissolved: boil rapidly for 1–2 minutes.

Turn the Sally Lunns out on to a wire rack and, while still warm, brush the tops with the sugar.

Buns and scones/1

Drop scones

Oven scones

Girdle scones

Scones are quick and easy to make. They should be soft and light as a sponge, and oven-fresh, so there should be no delay between making and baking. They are ideal for tea, served toasted and hot, or fresh with butter or thick cream and home-made preserves.

Many traditional scones are baked on a griddle or girdle. This is a thick, round iron plate, usually with a half-hoop handle. It is heated on top of the cooker, and the correct heat is important – if too hot, the outside crust of the scones becomes too brown, leaving the centre uncooked. To test for correct heat, sprinkle a little flour on the surface; it should turn light brown in 3 minutes.

Teabreads, halfway between a bread and a cake, are also popular for tea, as they keep well and can be made in advance. Soda bread is a good substitute for yeast bread in an emergency, and can be made shortly before it is required.

Drop Scones

PREPARATION TIME: *5 min.*
COOKING TIME: *3–5 min. per batch*

INGREDIENTS *(for 15–18 scones):*
4 oz. self-raising flour
Pinch of salt
1 level tablespoon caster sugar
1 egg
About ¼ pint milk
Lard for cooking

Set a griddle, heavy-based frying pan or hot-plate over heat. While it is warming, sift the flour and salt into a bowl and stir in the sugar. Make a well in the centre and drop in the egg; gradually add the milk, working in the flour with a spoon until a smooth batter is formed.

Grease the heated surface lightly with a little lard. When a slight haze appears, pour on small rounds of batter, well apart, either from a jug or with a spoon to give perfect rounds. As soon as the scones are puffed, bubbling on the surface and golden on the undersides, turn them over with a palette knife to brown on the other side. Serve at once, or place the scones between folds in a clean tea towel until serving time.

COOKING DROP SCONES

Pour batter on to greased griddle

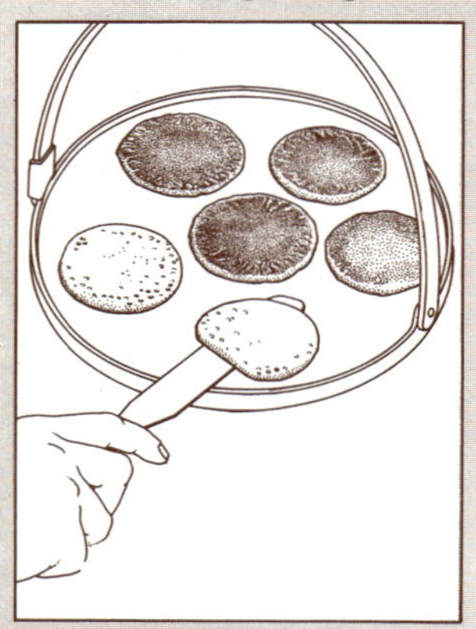

Turn over half-cooked scones

Oven Scones

PREPARATION TIME: *15 min.*
COOKING TIME: *10 min.*

INGREDIENTS *(for 10–12 scones):*
8 oz. plain flour
Pinch of salt
½ level teaspoon bicarbonate of soda
1 level teaspoon cream of tartar
1½ oz. firm margarine
About 4 tablespoons each milk and water mixed
Milk for glazing

Sift together the flour, salt, bicarbonate of soda and cream of tartar into a wide bowl. Cut up the margarine and rub it into the flour. Gradually add the milk and water and mix with a round-bladed knife to give a soft but manageable dough.

Knead the dough quickly on a lightly floured surface, to remove all cracks. Roll the dough out ½ in. thick, and cut out 2 in. rounds with a plain or fluted pastry cutter. Knead the trimmings together, roll them out and cut out as many scones as possible. Set the scones on a heated, ungreased baking tray, brush them with milk and bake them near the top of a pre-heated oven at 450°F (mark 8) for about 10 minutes, until well risen and light golden brown.

Girdle Scones

PREPARATION TIME: *5 min.*
COOKING TIME: *10 min.*

INGREDIENTS *(for 12 scones):*
8 oz. plain flour
1 level teaspoon bicarbonate of soda
2 level teaspoons cream of tartar
½ level teaspoon salt
1 oz. lard or firm margarine
1 oz. caster sugar
About ¼ pint milk

Heat a griddle, hot-plate or a heavy-based frying pan. Sift the flour, bicarbonate of soda, cream of tartar and salt into a bowl; cut up the lard and rub it into the flour with the fingertips until the mixture resembles fine breadcrumbs. Stir in the sugar, and gradually add the milk, mixing the dough with a round-bladed knife until soft but manageable.

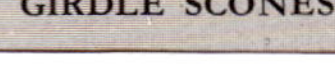

GIRDLE SCONES

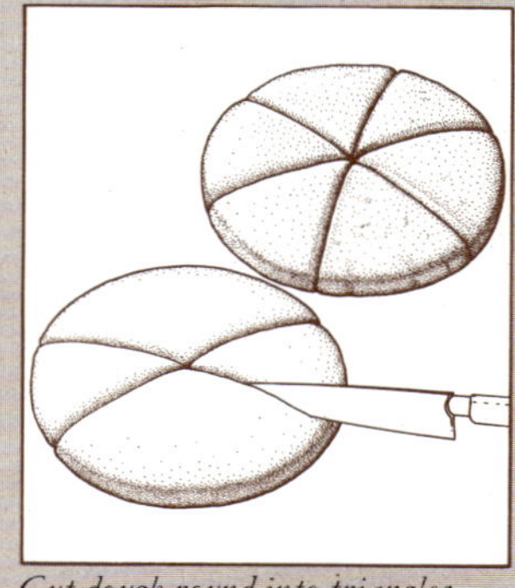

Cut dough round into triangles

Cook scones on greased griddle

Divide the dough in half. Knead each piece lightly and roll into two flat rounds, ¼–½ in. thick. Cut each round into six even triangles and cook on the greased griddle until evenly brown on one side, then turn and cook on the second side; allow about 5 minutes for each side. Cool on a wire rack.

Cheese Scones
PREPARATION TIME: *10 min.*
COOKING TIME: *15 min.*

INGREDIENTS *(for 12 scones)*:
8 oz. plain flour
½ level teaspoon salt
2½ level teaspoons baking powder
2 oz. butter or firm margarine
4 oz. grated Cheddar cheese
About ¼ pint milk

Sift together the flour, salt and baking powder. Mix the butter into the flour until it resembles fine breadcrumbs. Blend in the cheese. Gradually add the milk, mixing it with a round-bladed knife until the dough is soft and manageable.

Turn the dough on to a lightly floured surface, divide into two equal portions and knead them lightly with the fingertips. Shape each portion into a round, ¾ in. thick. Cut each round into six triangular portions and set them on a greased baking tray; prick the top with a fork.

Bake the scones in the centre of a pre-heated oven at 425°F (mark 7) for 12–15 minutes. Cool slightly before serving.

Sweet Sultana Scones
PREPARATION TIME: *15 min.*
COOKING TIME: *10 min.*

INGREDIENTS *(for 12 scones)*:
8 oz. plain flour
½ level teaspoon bicarbonate of soda
½ level teaspoon cream of tartar
Pinch of salt
1½ oz. firm margarine
1 oz. caster sugar
2 oz. sultanas
About ¼ pint soured milk or buttermilk
Milk for glazing

Sift together the flour, bicarbonate of soda, cream of tartar and salt. Cut up the margarine and rub it into the flour with the fingertips until the mixture resembles fine breadcrumbs. Add the sugar and sultanas. Gradually add the soured milk (prepare this by mixing ½ tablespoon fresh lemon juice into ¼ pint milk). Mix to a light, manageable dough, using a round-bladed knife.

Turn the dough on to a lightly floured surface and knead lightly until smooth. Roll out ½ in. thick and cut out the scones with a 2 in. plain or fluted pastry cutter. Re-knead the trimmings lightly to cut more scones. Set on an ungreased heated baking tray, brush the tops with milk and bake near the top of a pre-heated oven at 450°F (mark 8) for about 10 minutes.

Cool on a wire rack.

Wholemeal Scone Round
PREPARATION TIME: *10 min.*
COOKING TIME: *15 min.*

INGREDIENTS:
2 oz. plain flour
3 level teaspoons baking powder
Pinch of salt
6 oz. plain wholemeal flour
2 oz. firm margarine
2 oz. caster sugar
About ¼ pint milk

Sift the flour, baking powder and salt into a mixing bowl. Blend in the wholemeal flour and cut the margarine into knobs; rub this into the flour with the fingertips, until the mixture resembles fine breadcrumbs. Mix in the sugar. Add sufficient milk to give a light, soft dough, using a round-bladed knife for mixing.

Turn the dough on to a lightly floured surface. Knead it lightly until smooth, then shape it into a flat round, 6 in. wide. Mark it into six equal triangles with the back of a floured knife blade.

Set the scone round on a heated, lightly floured baking tray and bake near the top of the oven, pre-heated to 450°F (mark 8), for about 15 minutes.

Serve the scones warm, split and liberally buttered.

Singin' Hinny
This Northumberland girdle cake hisses or sings when it is cooking, hence the name.

PREPARATION TIME: *10 min.*
COOKING TIME: *10 min.*

INGREDIENTS:
12 oz. plain flour
1 level teaspoon salt
2 level teaspoons baking powder
2 oz. ground rice
2 oz. caster sugar
2 oz. lard
3 oz. currants
¼ pint milk
¼ pint single cream

Heat a griddle, heavy-based frying pan or hot-plate. Sift the flour, salt and baking powder into a bowl, then stir in the ground rice and sugar. Cut up the lard and rub it into the dry ingredients with the fingertips until the mixture resembles fine breadcrumbs. Stir in the currants and gradually work in the milk and cream mixed together, using a round-bladed knife. Beat the dough lightly until soft and manageable.

Turn the dough on to a floured surface and pat or roll it out into a large round, ¼ in. thick, or into 3 small rounds. Prick the top with a fork and put the cakes on the greased griddle.

Cook over low heat for about 5 minutes, then turn the cakes carefully with a palette knife and cook until golden.

Slice the singin' hinny into halves and butter liberally, then sandwich together and serve while still warm.

Soda Bread
PREPARATION TIME: *15 min.*
COOKING TIME: *30 min.*

INGREDIENTS:
1 lb. plain flour
2 level teaspoons bicarbonate of soda
2 level teaspoons cream of tartar
1 level teaspoon salt
1 oz. lard
1–2 level teaspoons caster sugar (optional)
½ pint soured milk, or 9 fluid oz. buttermilk made up to ½ pint with milk

Sift the flour, bicarbonate of soda, cream of tartar and salt into a bowl. Cut up the lard and rub it into the flour with the fingertips until the mixture resembles fine breadcrumbs. Mix in the sugar if used. Make a well in the centre of the flour, add the milk (soured with 1 tablespoon of lemon juice) or the buttermilk, and mix to a soft but manageable dough, working the ingredients with a round-bladed knife. Add more milk if necessary.

Turn the dough on to a floured surface, knead it lightly and shape it into a 7 in. round; flatten it slightly. Mark the round into four with the back of a knife, set it on a floured baking tray and bake in the centre of a pre-heated oven at 400°F (mark 6) for about 30 minutes.

Cool on a wire rack and serve fresh, as a teabread.

Buns and scones/2

Cheese scones

Sweet sultana scones

Wholemeal scone round

Singin' Hinny

Soda bread

Buns and scones/ 3

Welsh cakes

Bran teabread

Rock buns

Raspberry buns

Apple cakes

Welsh Cakes

PREPARATION TIME: *15 min.*
COOKING TIME: *25 min.*

INGREDIENTS *(for 16 cakes)*:
8 oz. plain flour
1 level teaspoon baking powder
Pinch of salt
1½–2 oz. butter or firm margarine
1½–2 oz. lard
3 oz. caster sugar
2–3 oz. currants
1 egg
About 2 tablespoons milk

Heat a griddle, heavy-based frying pan or hot-plate. Sift the flour, baking powder and salt into a bowl; cut up the butter and lard and rub into the flour with the fingertips until the mixture resembles fine breadcrumbs. Stir in the sugar and currants. Beat the egg lightly and add it to the flour mixture, with just enough milk to give a firm paste similar to shortcrust pastry.

Roll the dough ¼ in. thick, on a floured surface, and cut out rounds using a 3 in. plain or fluted pastry cutter. Bake the cakes on the greased griddle, over low heat for about 3 minutes on each side, until golden brown. Cool on a wire rack, and serve with a dusting of caster sugar.

Bran Teabread

PREPARATION TIME: *10 min.*
RESTING TIME: *8 hours*
COOKING TIME: *1¼–1½ hours*

INGREDIENTS:
3 oz. All Bran
8 oz. sultanas
8 oz. light soft brown sugar
½ pint milk
6 oz. self-raising flour
1 level teaspoon baking powder

Mix the All Bran, sultanas, sugar and milk in a bowl and leave to stand overnight, covered with a cloth.

Grease and line a loaf tin (9 in. by 5 in. top measurements). Sift the flour and baking powder into the soaked ingredients, blend thoroughly and spoon into the prepared tin. Level the top of the mixture and bake in the centre of a pre-heated oven, at 375°F (mark 5), for about 1¼ hours until the bread is well risen and just firm to the touch. If the loaf browns too quickly, cover it with a double sheet of greaseproof paper.

Turn out the loaf, remove the paper and cool on a wire rack. Serve the loaf sliced and buttered. It is best left for a day or two to mature before serving, and will keep for 1 week in a tin.

Rock Buns

PREPARATION TIME: *15 min.*
COOKING TIME: *15 min.*

INGREDIENTS *(for 12 buns)*:
8 oz. plain flour
Pinch of salt
2 level teaspoons baking powder
2 oz. butter or margarine
2 oz. lard or whipped-up fat
4 oz. mixed dried fruit
4 oz. Demerara sugar
Grated rind of half lemon
1 large egg
1–2 tablespoons milk

Grease two baking trays. Sift together the flour, salt and baking powder into a bowl. Rub the fat into the flour until the mixture resembles fine breadcrumbs. Stir in the fruit, sugar and lemon rind. Beat the egg with 1 tablespoon of milk. Using a fork, stir the egg mixture into the dry ingredients, adding a little more milk if necessary to give a stiff dough – the mixture should just knit together.

Using two forks, place the mixture in 12 small heaps on the greased baking trays. Keep the mixture rough to give a rocky appearance which will remain after baking. Bake just above the centre of the oven, pre-heated to 400°F (mark 6), for 15–20 minutes, or until golden brown. Cool on a wire rack and serve the rock buns fresh.

Raspberry Buns

PREPARATION TIME: *25 min.*
COOKING TIME: *10–15 min.*

INGREDIENTS *(for 10 buns)*:
7 oz. self-raising flour
Pinch of salt
1 oz. ground rice
3 oz. caster sugar
3 oz. butter or margarine
1 egg
1 tablespoon milk
Raspberry jam
Beaten egg

Grease two baking trays. In a bowl, sift together the flour, salt, ground rice and sugar. Add the fat, cut in small pieces, and rub into the flour with the fingertips until the mixture resembles fine breadcrumbs. Beat the egg lightly with the milk and mix this in with a round-bladed knife, until the mixture forms a light and manageable dough.

Shape the dough between the palms of the hands into 10 even-sized balls. Make a hole with a floured finger in the centre of each ball and drop in a little raspberry jam. Close up the opening, pinching the edges together.

Place the buns well apart on the baking trays, as they double in size when baked. Brush with beaten egg and bake just above the centre of the oven pre-heated to 425°F (mark 7) for 10–15 minutes. Cool on a wire rack.

Apple Cakes

PREPARATION TIME: *30 min.*
COOKING TIME: *15 min.*

INGREDIENTS *(for 16 cakes)*:
1 lb. cooking apples
Brown sugar
8 oz. plain flour
2 level teaspoons cream of tartar
1 level teaspoon bicarbonate of soda
Pinch of salt
4 oz. margarine
4 oz. caster sugar
1 egg
Caster sugar for dusting

Grease 16 patty tins thoroughly. Peel and core the apples and cook them, with brown sugar to taste, over low heat until they form a thick purée.

Meanwhile, sift together the flour, cream of tartar, bicarbonate of soda and salt. Cut the margarine into small pieces and rub this into the flour until the mixture resembles fine breadcrumbs. Stir in sugar and mix in the beaten egg to form a soft but manageable dough. Knead lightly on a floured surface and roll out, ⅛ in. thick. Handle the dough carefully, as it crumbles easily. Cut out 16 bases and 16 lids with a plain 2½ in. wide pastry cutter. If necessary, knead the trimmings and roll out more shapes.

Lift the cake bases into the tins with a palette knife. Cover with a teaspoonful of the apple purée and top with a lid – this seals itself during cooking. Sprinkle the tops with caster sugar. Bake just above the centre of the oven, pre-heated to 400°F (mark 6), for about 15 minutes. Leave to cool slightly in the tins, then ease the cakes out with a palette knife and cool completely on a wire rack. Serve while still fresh.

Biscuits

1 GINGER DROPS p.44
2 SHORT FINGERS p.43
3 BRANDY SNAPS p.43
4 MACAROONS p.43
5 JUMBLES p.42
6 ORANGE CREAMS p.42
7 BOSTON BROWNIES p.44
8 LEMON MELTAWAYS p.42
9 SHORTBREAD p.44
10 REFRIGERATOR COOKIES p.45

Bread, Buns and Scones

1 LARDY CAKE p.39
2 OVEN SCONES p.20
3 SODA BREAD p.21
4 CHELSEA BUNS p.41
5 BRIOCHES p.40
6 SALLY LUNN p.19
7 CROWN LOAF p.17
8 FLOWERPOT LOAF p.18
9 SINGIN' HINNY p.21
10 GIRDLE SCONES p.20
11 COB LOAF p.17
12 DANISH PASTRIES p.39
13 POPPY SEED PLAIT p.18
14 APRICOT AND WALNUT LOAF p.19

Bread, Buns and Scones

Cakes and Sponges

Cakes and Sponges

1 VICTORIA SANDWICH p.32
2 CHOCOLATE LAYER CAKE p.32
3 PINEAPPLE AND CHERRY LOAF p.33
4 DUNDEE CAKE p.34
5 SWISS ROLL p.34
6 GENOESE SPONGE p.35
7 GINGERBREAD p.35
8 MADEIRA CAKE p.32
9 COCONUT CASTLES p.33

Confectionery

1 CHOCOLATE-COVERED PINEAPPLE p.46
2 STUFFED DATES p.47
3 GINGER MARZIPAN p.47
4 CHOCOLATE FUDGE p.46
5 PEANUT BRITTLE p.47
6 CHOCOLATE-COVERED DATES p.46
7 MARZIPAN CONFECTIONERY p.47
8 ALMOND PETITS FOURS p.47
9 COCONUT ICE p.46
10 COLLETTES p.46
11 PEPPERMINT CREAMS p.47
12 RUM TRUFFLES p.47

Cakes/ 1

Ingredients

The key to successful cake-making lies in following the recipe in detail, and in understanding the reaction of the various ingredients to each other. The basic ingredients are fat, flour, raising agents, eggs, sugar and often fruit. Using the right size tins, correct oven position and temperature are also important factors.

Basically cakes fall into two categories: those made with fat, and the sponge types made without fat. The exception to sponge mixtures is the Genoese sponge which combines the two methods.

In fat-type cakes, the fat is either rubbed in, creamed or melted. Rubbed-in mixtures are generally used for plain, everyday cakes, such as Tyrol cake, while creamed cakes are rich and soft with a fairly close even grain and soft crumb as in a Victoria sandwich.

In melted cakes, e.g. gingerbread, the fat, often with liquid, sugar, syrup or treacle added, is poured into the dry ingredients to give a batter-like consistency. Mix cakes by hand or use an electric mixer after incorporating the flour with fat and eggs.

Preparations

Always use the right size tin. Bigger, smaller or shallower tins than those called for can cause a cake to fail. If the tin is of incorrect size, fill to only half its depth so that the cake will rise to, but not above, the top. Test frequently to see if the cakes are cooked. Prepare the tin either by lining or by greasing with butter and sprinkling with flour. Set the oven to the correct temperature if the cake is to be baked at once after mixing, and assemble the necessary ingredients – eggs, butter and firm margarine should be at room temperature.

Fats

Butter, margarine, whipped-up white fat, lard and corn oil are all used in cakes. However, they are not always interchangeable.

Butter gives the best flavour and improves the keeping quality of cakes, but firm margarine can be used in place of butter in most recipes, with only a slight difference in flavour. Soft table margarine, sold in tubs, is composed of blended oils; it is particularly suitable for cakes where all the ingredients are mixed in one operation.

Whipped-up white fat is light and easy to blend with other ingredients. Like lard, this fat contains little or no salt and is almost 100 per cent fat; both can be used interchangeably in recipes.

Corn oil is suitable for most recipes using melted fat, but it is advisable to follow the manufacturer's instructions, as the characteristics of oils vary. It is easy to mix in and gives a soft texture, but the cakes do not keep quite so well.

Flour

Plain or self-raising flour or a mixture of both are used for cakes. Whichever type of flour is used, it should always be sifted with a pinch of salt. Salt is added not only for flavour, but because of its chemical effect in toughening up the soft mixture of fat and sugar.

Self-raising flour is popular, as it eliminates errors in calculating the exact amount of raising agents, which are already evenly blended throughout the flour.

A mixture of plain and self-raising flour is ideal for rich cakes which would rise too much if self-raising flour only were used. Other cakes, and in particular whisked cakes such as sponges, should be made only with plain flour, as they have their own natural raising agent – air.

In some melted cakes plain flour is mixed with bicarbonate of soda. These cakes contain treacle, which on its own is slightly acid and must be offset by an alkali to act as a raising agent.

Raising Agents

Baking powder is a ready-made blend of soda and cream of tartar, and these together form carbon dioxide. The rubbery substance in flour – known as gluten – is capable, when wet, of suspending carbon dioxide in the form of tiny bubbles.

Since all gases expand when heated, these bubbles become larger during baking, and thus cause a cake to rise.

However, cake mixtures can hold only a certain amount of gas, and if too much raising agent is used the cake will rise well at first, but later collapse, and this results in a heavy, close texture. A combination of cream of tartar and bicarbonate of soda is sometimes used as an alternative to baking powder, in the proportion of 2:1.

Eggs

These give lightness to cake mixtures, as they expand on heating and trap the air beaten into the mixture. When whisked egg is used in a cake mixture, air instead of carbon dioxide causes it to rise.

Cakes with a high proportion of egg, such as sponge cakes, need little if any raising agent.

In creamed mixtures, the eggs are beaten in, not whisked, and a little additional raising agent is required. In plain cakes, where beaten egg is added with the liquid, the egg helps to bind the mixture but does not act as the main raising agent.

Sugar

Granulated sugar is the least expensive white sugar; it can be used in rubbed-in cakes, but as it is coarse it may give a spotted appearance to the cake crust. Caster sugar, being finer, creams more easily with fats and gives a finer, softer cake.

Demerara sugar should only be used in recipes for melted cakes, where sugar is dissolved, unless otherwise recommended.

Soft brown sugar, medium or light brown in colour, is good for rubbed-in, melted and fruit cakes. The colour and flavour add richness and the soft, moist quality helps to keep certain cakes in good condition longer.

Barbados sugar, very dark brown, full-flavoured and moist, is used in rich fruit mixtures for wedding and birthday cakes. Syrup, honey and treacle, often combined with sugar, are used to sweeten, colour and flavour cakes such as gingerbread. They give a close, moist texture.

Fruit and Peel

Always choose good-quality dried fruit. Stored sultanas sometimes become hard, but they can be plumped up in hot water, and thoroughly drained and dried.

Sultanas can be bought ready-washed or unwashed. Unwashed are cheaper, but the fruit should be washed well, drained and left to dry thoroughly before use. Alternatively, clean sultanas by rubbing in a sieve with a little

Cakes/2

Preparing cake tins

Lining a rectangular tin

Lining a round cake tin

Oven positions

Cooling cakes

Storing cakes

flour to remove the stalks.

Seedless raisins are similar in size to sultanas, but ready-prepared seeded or stoned raisins are large and juicy. To remove the stones from a raisin, work it between the finger-tips to ease out the stones, occasionally dipping the fingers in water. Wash any syrup from glacé cherries and dry them thoroughly.

Peel can be bought ready-chopped, but make sure that it looks soft and moist. Coarsely chopped, thin cut peel sometimes needs more chopping to make it finer. 'Caps' of candied orange, lemon, grapefruit and citron peel should be stripped of sugar before being shredded, grated, minced or chopped.

Preparing Cake Tins

All cakes should be baked in tins that have been greased, greased and floured, sugared or lined with paper. The appearance of a finished cake depends largely on the expert preparation of the cake tin.

Sandwich tins and cake tins for rubbed-in mixtures are often greased only by brushing melted white fat evenly over the inside. But as an extra precaution against sticking and for ease of turning out, a paper liner of greased greaseproof fitted into the base is a good idea. The paper does not necessarily have to reach the edge of the tin but the centre must be covered.

For fatless sponges, flour the greased tin to give an extra crisp crust, or dust it with flour, blended with an equal amount of sugar. Shake the dusting mixture round the tin until evenly coated, and remove any excess by gently tapping the inverted tin.

For baking small cakes or buns, fluted paper cups set in patty tins are by far the easiest to use; otherwise grease the patty pans thoroughly.

Non-stick paper can be used instead of greaseproof paper to line both round and rectangular tins. Tins with a non-stick surface need no greasing or lining, but a paper lining helps to protect against a solid crust, especially during long baking. For cakes baked in non-stick tins, the baking time should be reduced by a few minutes as these tins brown the contents more quickly.

Lining a Rectangular Tin

Measure the length and width of the tin and add twice the tin's depth to each of these measurements. Cut a rectangle of greaseproof paper to this size and place the tin squarely in the centre. At each corner, make a cut from the angle of the paper as far as the corner of the tin.

Grease the inside of the tin and put in the paper so that it fits, closely overlapping at the corners. Brush again with melted fat.

Lining a Round Cake Tin

Cut a strip of greaseproof paper as long as the circumference of the tin and 2 in. wider than the depth of the tin. Make a fold about 1 in. deep along one of the long edges, and cut this at $\frac{1}{2}$ in. intervals up to the fold, at a slight angle. Curve the strip round and slip it around the sides of the greased tin, nicked fold downwards so that this lies flat against the base of the tin.

Cut a circle of paper slightly smaller than the bottom of the tin and drop it in over the nicked paper. Brush with melted fat. For rich cakes with long cooking times, double-line the tin.

Oven Positions

In gas cookers, the hottest shelf is at the top, but in electric cookers the heat is more evenly distributed. A cake is generally baked in the centre of the oven.

When baking two cakes, place them side by side but do not let them touch the sides of the oven or each other. If the tins are too large, bake the cakes on two oven shelves but avoid placing the tins directly over each other, and switch the tins over when the cake mixture has set.

Small cakes are usually baked above the centre, but not at the top of the oven. Place the tins or patty pans on baking trays before putting them in the oven.

Cooling Cakes

With only a few exceptions, all cakes should be thoroughly cooled before being cut, frosted or stored. After baking, most cakes are best left to settle in their tins for 5–10 minutes before being turned out. Large cakes and rich fruit cakes are often left to get lukewarm before turning them out.

Run a spatula, small palette knife or round-bladed knife around the edge of the cake (do not use metal tools on non-stick tins). Place a wire rack over the cake and invert both the cake and rack, then lift the tin carefully. The lining paper may be peeled off or left on. Turn the cake with the aid of a second rack or the hand so that the top is uppermost. Leave the cake to cool completely on the wire rack. To prevent the wire mesh marking the surface of a soft-textured cake place a tea towel over the rack before turning the cake out.

Storing Cakes

Storage time depends on the type of cake. Generally, iced cakes stay fresh longer than un-iced cakes, and the more fat in the cake mixture the longer it keeps. Fatless sponges should preferably be eaten on the day of baking as they go stale quickly.

Store both plain and iced cakes in airtight cake tins or similar containers. Cream-filled cakes are best kept in the refrigerator. Wrap fruit cakes with the lining paper left on in kitchen foil before storing. If slightly warm when wrapped they retain the moisture better.

Most cakes also store well in the home freezer.

TURNING OUT CAKES

Run knife along inner edge of tin

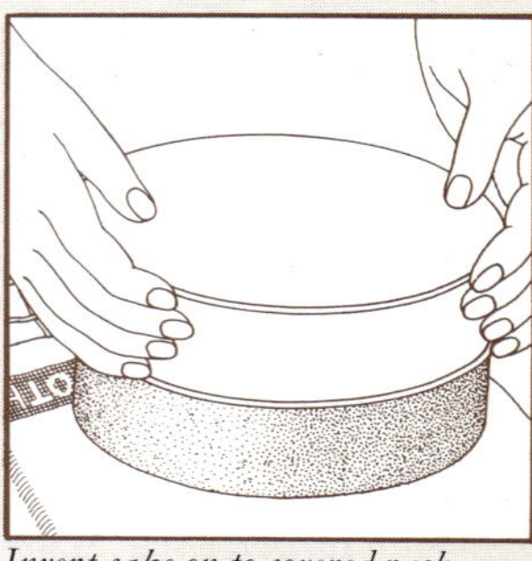

Invert cake on to covered rack

RUBBED-IN CAKES

These plain cakes are the easiest of all to make. As the proportion of fat to flour is half or less, rubbed-in mixtures are best eaten when fresh or within 2–3 days of baking. Rubbing in consists of blending flour and fat to a crumb-like mixture, using the tips of the fingers.

To keep the mixture cool, raise the hands high when letting the crumbs drop back into the bowl. Shake the bowl occasionally to bring bigger crumbs to the surface. Make sure the texture is even, but do not handle more than necessary, or the crumbs will toughen and the fat become soft and oily.

The amount of liquid added can be critical: too much results in a doughy texture, whereas too little gives a crumbly cake which quickly dries out. For a large cake, the mixture should only just drop off the spoon when gently tapped.

Tyrol Cake

PREPARATION TIME: *25 min.*
COOKING TIME: *1¾ hours*

INGREDIENTS:
8 oz. plain flour
Pinch of salt
1 level teaspoon ground cinnamon
3½ oz. margarine
2 oz. caster sugar
2 oz. currants
2 oz. sultanas
1 level teaspoon bicarbonate of soda
¼ pint milk
3 level tablespoons clear honey

Grease a 6 in. round cake tin. Sift the flour, salt and cinnamon into a bowl, cut up the margarine and rub into the flour until the mixture resembles fine breadcrumbs. Stir in the sugar, currants and sultanas and make a well in the centre. Dissolve the bicarbonate of soda in the milk, stir in the honey and pour this mixture into the well in the flour. Using a wooden spoon, gradually work in the dry ingredients, adding more milk if necessary to give a firm dropping consistency.

Spoon the cake mixture into the prepared tin and level the top. Bake in the centre of the oven, pre-heated to 325°F (mark 3), for 1¾–2 hours or until well risen.

Test with a fine skewer – if it comes away clean, the cake is cooked. Cool on a wire rack.

Strawberry Shortcake

PREPARATION TIME: *25 min.*
COOKING TIME: *20 min.*

INGREDIENTS:
8 oz. plain flour
1 level teaspoon cream of tartar
½ level teaspoon bicarbonate of soda
Pinch of salt
2 oz. butter or margarine
1½ oz. caster sugar
1 egg
3–4 tablespoons milk
FILLING:
½ lb. hulled strawberries
½ pint double cream
1 tablespoon milk
Caster sugar
Butter

Sift together the flour, cream of tartar, bicarbonate of soda and salt into a bowl. Cut the butter into small pieces and rub into the flour until the mixture resembles fine breadcrumbs. Blend in the sugar. Make a well in the centre, stir in the beaten egg and enough milk to give a soft but manageable dough. Knead lightly on a floured surface, then roll the dough out into a 7 in. circle.

Place on a greased baking tray, dust lightly with flour and bake towards the top of an oven pre-heated to 425°F (mark 7) for about 20 minutes. Cool slightly on a wire rack.

STRAWBERRY SHORTCAKE

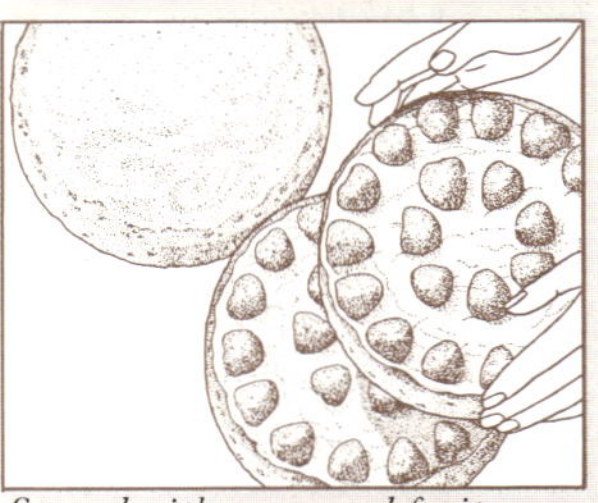

Spread with cream and fruit

Decorate top with piped cream

For the filling, slice the strawberries thickly. Whisk together the cream and the milk, sweetened with caster sugar to taste, until it holds its shape. Cut the warm shortcake into three layers, horizontally, with a serrated knife, and lightly butter each. Spread the cream over all three circles, then top with the sliced strawberries and sandwich the cake together. Decorate the top with piped cream.

Cherry and Coconut Cake

PREPARATION TIME: *30 min.*
COOKING TIME: *1¼ hours*

INGREDIENTS:
12 oz. self-raising flour
Pinch of salt
6 oz. margarine
8 oz. glacé cherries
2 oz. desiccated coconut
6 oz. caster sugar
2 large eggs
¼ pint milk
Granulated sugar

Grease a 7½–8 in. round cake tin. Sift the flour and salt into a bowl, and rub in the cut-up margarine. Quarter the cherries, toss them in the coconut and add, with the sugar, to the flour, stirring lightly to combine. Beat the eggs and stir into the mixture, together with sufficient milk to give a stiff but dropping consistency.

Turn the mixture into the prepared tin, level the surface, dust with granulated sugar and bake in the centre of the oven pre-heated to 350°F (mark 4) for about 1¼ hours or until well risen and golden brown. Cool on a wire rack.

CREAMED CAKES

These are all made from the basic method of blending fat with sugar. Put the cut up butter or margarine into a bowl large enough to allow the fat – and sugar – to be beaten vigorously without overflowing. With a wooden spoon, beat the fat against the sides of the bowl until soft; add the sugar and beat or cream the mixture until fluffy and pale yellow. After 7–10 minutes the volume should have increased greatly and the mixture should drop easily from the spoon. Eggs may be added whole or beaten.

If an electric mixer is used, set the dial at the speed suggested in the manufacturer's instructions,

Cakes/4

Victoria sandwich

Chocolate layer cake

Madeira cake

and allow 3–4 minutes for beating. Switch off the mixer from time to time and scrape the cake mixture down into the bowl.

Victoria Sandwich

PREPARATION TIME: *15 min.*
COOKING TIME: *25 min.*

INGREDIENTS:
4 oz. butter or margarine
4 oz. caster sugar
2 large eggs
Vanilla essence
or grated lemon or orange rind
4 oz. self-raising flour

Grease two 7 in. straight-sided sandwich tins and line the bases with buttered greaseproof paper. In a bowl, beat the butter until soft, then add the sugar and cream until light and fluffy. Beat in the eggs, one at a time, then add a few drops of vanilla essence or finely grated lemon or orange rind. Beat in the sifted flour.

Divide this mixture equally between the two tins, and level off the surface. Bake the cakes side by side, if possible, in the centre of the oven pre-heated to 350°F (mark 4) for about 25 minutes. Cool on a wire rack.

Layer the cakes with jam or a butter cream filling. Dust top with caster or sifted icing sugar or cover with soft icing.

Chocolate Layer Cake

PREPARATION TIME: *25 min.*
COOKING TIME: *30 min.*

INGREDIENTS:
4 oz. butter or margarine
4 oz. caster sugar
2 large eggs
2 level tablespoons cocoa
4 oz. self-raising flour
Pinch of salt
FILLING:
1½ oz. butter or margarine
3 oz. icing sugar
2 teaspoons coffee essence
1 tablespoon top of the milk

Grease a straight-sided 8 in. wide sandwich tin and line with paper, cutting the band of paper to come ½ in. above the rim. Grease the paper lining.

Beat the butter until soft, then add the sugar and cream the mixture until light and fluffy. Beat the eggs before beating them into the mixture, a little at a time. In a small bowl or cup, blend the cocoa with enough cold water to make a paste. Lightly beat this into the creamed mixture, alternately with the sifted flour and salt. Turn the cake mixture into the prepared tin, level the surface and bake in the centre of a pre-heated oven at 350°F (mark 4) for about 30 minutes or until well risen and spongy to the touch.

Meanwhile, make the filling. Beat the butter until soft and creamy, sift the icing sugar and add a little at a time. Stir in the coffee essence and milk.

Turn the cake on to a wire rack, and remove the lining paper. Cut the cold cake in half horizontally, and spread the bottom half with the filling; place the top in position and lightly press the two halves together. Dust the top with sifted icing sugar. Using the back of a knife blade, draw a lattice pattern across the sugar.

CREAMED CAKE MIXTURE

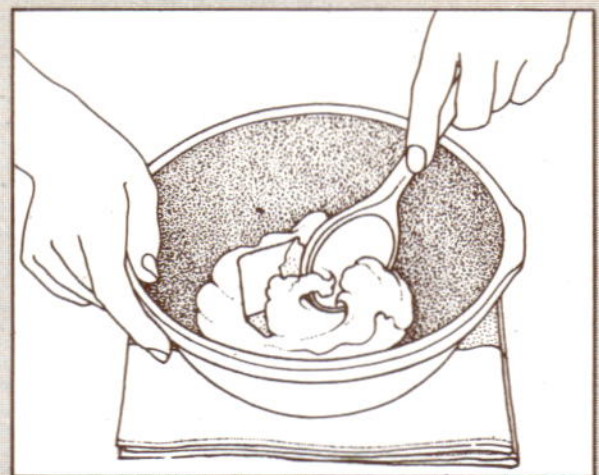
Stand bowl on damp cloth

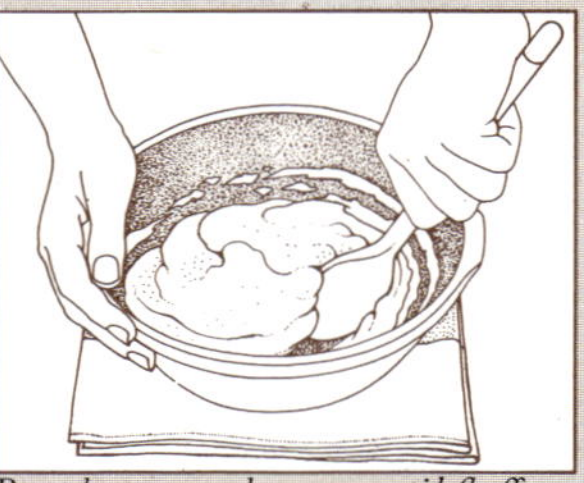
Beat butter and sugar until fluffy

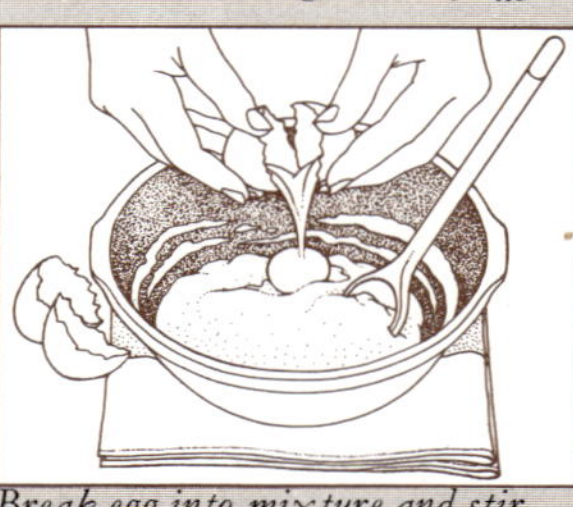
Break egg into mixture and stir

Alternatively, add beaten egg

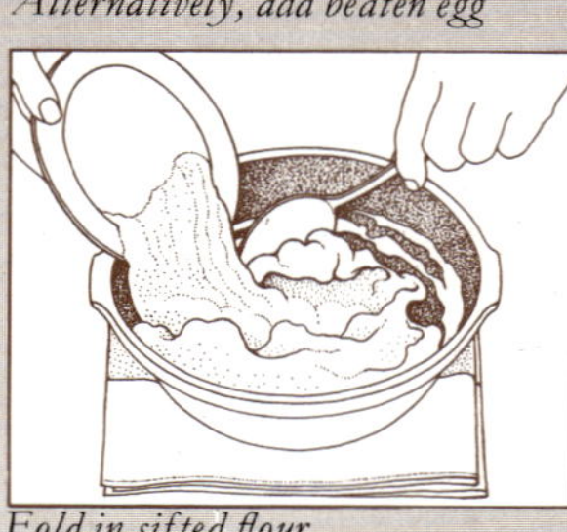
Fold in sifted flour

CHOCOLATE LAYER CAKE

Sift icing sugar over layered cake

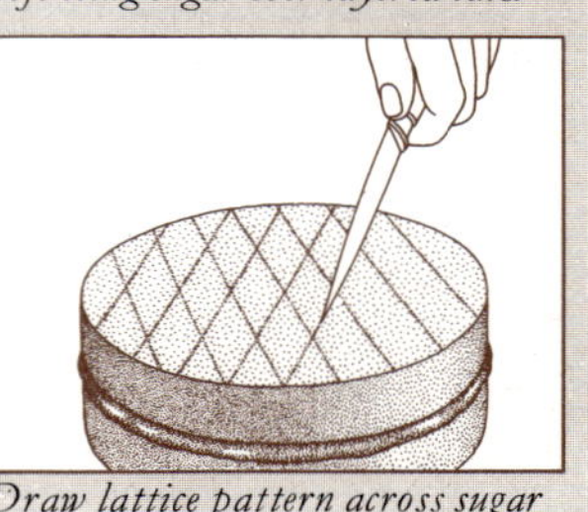
Draw lattice pattern across sugar

Madeira Cake

PREPARATION TIME: *20 min.*
COOKING TIME: *1–1¼ hours*

INGREDIENTS:
6 oz. butter or margarine
6 oz. caster sugar
3 large eggs
5 oz. self-raising flour
4 oz. plain flour
Pinch of salt
Grated rind and juice of half lemon
Citron peel

Grease a 7 in. round cake tin and line with greaseproof paper. Beat the butter until soft, then add the sugar and cream until light and fluffy. Add the eggs, one at a time, beating well between each addition. Fold in the sifted flours and salt, alternately with the strained lemon juice and rind. Turn the mixture into the prepared tin and level the surface. Arrange slices of thinly cut citron peel over the top.

Bake in the centre of an oven pre-heated to 325°F (mark 3) for 1–1¼ hours. Leave to cool in the tin for 10 minutes, then turn out on to a wire rack.

Pineapple and Cherry Loaf

PREPARATION TIME: *35 min.*
COOKING TIME: *1½ hours*

INGREDIENTS:
6 oz. glacé cherries
1½ oz. glacé pineapple
3 oz. ground almonds
Grated rind of half lemon
6 oz. butter or margarine
6 oz. caster sugar
3 eggs
3 oz. self-raising flour
3 oz. plain flour
Pinch of salt

Grease a loaf tin, 4½ in. by 9 in. (top measurement); line with buttered greaseproof paper. Wash and dry the cherries, cut them in half and set 10 aside. Chop the pineapple and mix with the cherries, ground almonds and lemon rind.

Beat the butter until soft, then add the sugar, and cream the mixture until light and fluffy. Beat the eggs before adding them to the mixture a little at a time. Sift and fold the flours and salt, a third at a time, into the creamed mixture. Lastly fold in the fruit.

Spoon into the prepared tin, level the surface and arrange the reserved cherries on top. Cover the tin loosely with kitchen foil, taking care that it does not touch the cake mixture. Bake in the centre of an oven pre-heated to 350°F (mark 4) for about 1½ hours or until well-risen and firm to the touch. Cool on a wire rack and remove the lining paper.

Coconut Castles

PREPARATION TIME: *20 min.*
COOKING TIME: *20 min.*

INGREDIENTS *(for 6–8 cakes)*:
4 oz. butter or margarine
4 oz. caster sugar
2 eggs
4 oz. self-raising flour
Pinch of salt
4 tablespoons red jam
1 tablespoon water
2 oz. desiccated coconut
6 glacé cherries
Angelica

Grease six dariole moulds. Beat the butter until soft, add the sugar, and cream until light and fluffy. Beat in the beaten eggs. Gradually fold in the sifted flour and salt. Divide the mixture evenly between the moulds, filling them no more than two-thirds full. Set on a baking tray and bake in the centre of an oven, pre-heated to 350°F (mark 4) for 20 minutes or until golden. Cool on a wire rack.

When the castles are cold, bring the jam and water to the boil and cook for 1 minute. Level the wide base of the castles if necessary, brush them all over with the jam and roll in coconut. Garnish with a cherry and angelica leaves.

Swiss Tarts

PREPARATION TIME: *25 min.*
COOKING TIME: *20 min.*

INGREDIENTS *(for 6 cakes)*:
4 oz. butter
1 oz. caster sugar
Vanilla essence
4 oz. plain flour
Icing sugar
Red currant jelly

Place 6 paper baking cases in a sheet of patty tins and set on a baking tray. Beat the butter until soft, add the sugar, and cream until light and fluffy. Beat in a few drops of vanilla essence and gradually add the flour, beating well between each addition.

Put the mixture in a fabric piping bag fitted with a large star vegetable nozzle. Pipe the mixture into the paper cases, starting at the centre, and piping with a spiral motion round the sides, leaving a shallow depression in the centre. Bake in the centre of an oven, pre-heated to 350°F (mark 4) for about 20 minutes or until set and tinged with colour.

Leave the cakes in their paper cases to cool on a wire rack. Dredge with icing sugar and top each tart with a little red currant jelly.

Farmhouse Fruit Cake

PREPARATION TIME: *10 min.*
COOKING TIME: *about 1½ hours*

INGREDIENTS:
6 oz. soft tub margarine
6 oz. caster sugar
3 oz. sultanas
3 oz. seedless raisins
3 oz. glacé cherries, chopped
12 oz. self-raising flour
Pinch of salt
1 level teaspoon mixed spice
3 tablespoons milk
3 eggs

Grease an 8 in. round cake tin and line with buttered greaseproof paper. Mix the margarine and all the dry ingredients in a bowl, then add the milk and eggs and beat with a wooden spoon until well mixed, for 2–3 minutes. Turn into the prepared tin and level the top.

Bake in the centre of the oven pre-heated to 350°F (mark 4) for about 1½ hours. When a warm skewer comes away clean, the cake is cooked. Leave the cake in the tin for 15 minutes before turning out on to a wire rack to cool.

Coffee Walnut Cake

PREPARATION TIME: *20 min.*
COOKING TIME: *35–40 min.*

INGREDIENTS:
4 oz. soft tub margarine
4 oz. caster sugar
2 large eggs
2 oz. chopped walnuts
1 tablespoon coffee essence
4 oz. self-raising flour
Pinch of salt
1 level teaspoon baking powder
FILLING:
3 oz. soft tub margarine
8 oz. icing sugar
2 teaspoons milk
2 teaspoons coffee essence
Walnut halves

Grease two 7 in. straight-sided sandwich tins, and line the bases with buttered greaseproof paper. Put the margarine and sugar, eggs, chopped walnuts and coffee essence in a bowl. Sift in the flour with the salt and baking powder. Beat these ingredients with a wooden spoon for 2–3 minutes or until well combined. Divide the mixture between the prepared tins, level the surface and bake in the centre of an oven, pre-heated to 325°F (mark 3), for 35–40 minutes, or until well-risen and spongy to the touch.

When baked, turn the cakes out on a wire rack to cool before removing the lining paper.

Meanwhile make the filling: beat the margarine, sifted icing sugar, milk and coffee essence in a bowl until smooth. Sandwich the cakes together with two-thirds of the filling, top with the remaining filling and mark the surface with the prongs of a fork in a decorative pattern. Place walnut halves on top of the cake.

Cakes/5

Cakes/6

Dundee cake

Whisked cakes

Strawberry cream sponge

Swiss roll

Dundee Cake

PREPARATION TIME: *20 min.*
COOKING TIME: *3½ hours*

INGREDIENTS:
8 oz. plain flour
Pinch of salt
8 oz. butter or margarine
8 oz. caster sugar
4 large eggs
12 oz. sultanas
12 oz. currants
6 oz. chopped mixed peel
4 oz. small glacé cherries
Grated rind of half lemon
2–3 oz. whole almonds

Grease an 8 in. round cake tin and line with double paper. Tie a band of brown paper round the outside of the tin and let it extend about 2 in. above the rim. Set the tin on a double piece of brown paper on a baking tray.

Sift together the flour and salt. Beat the butter until soft, add the sugar and cream until light and fluffy. Beat the eggs into the mixture, a little at a time. Fold in the flour and, when evenly combined, fold in the sultanas, currants, peel, cherries and lemon rind. Blanch the almonds, slip off the skins and chop 1 oz.; add to the cake mixture. Spoon into the tin.

BLANCHING WHOLE ALMONDS

Slide off softened skins

Split almonds in half

Split the rest of the almonds lengthways, and arrange them, rounded side up, over the levelled cake surface. Bake just below the centre of an oven, pre-heated to 300°F (mark 2), for about 3½ hours. If the cake shows signs of browning too quickly, cover the top with a sheet of damp greaseproof paper, and reduce the heat to 275°F (mark 1) for the last hour. Remove the cake from the oven when a skewer comes away clean from the cake.

Cool in the tin for 30 minutes, then turn out and cool on a wire rack. Wrap the cake in foil, with the lining paper in position. The cake is best kept for at least 1 week and up to 1 month to bring out the full flavour.

WHISKED CAKES

These are the lightest of all cake mixtures, their texture depending entirely on the incorporated eggs. The fatless cake mixture is used for sponges, which should be baked as soon as they are mixed.

Use a hand-operated, rotary or balloon whisk and to stabilise the mixture, place the deep bowl of eggs and sugar over hot, not boiling, water. Do not let the mixture become too hot or the sponge will have a tough texture. For a maximum rise, the mixture should be thick enough to leave a trail when the whisk is lifted. If an electric mixer is used, it is unnecessary to heat the bowl.

Blending in the flour is another important step. Sift the flour two or three times, the last time over the whisked egg mixture, then fold it carefully into the mixture without flattening the bulk. Use a metal spoon or plastic spatula in a figure-of-eight movement.

Strawberry Cream Sponge

PREPARATION TIME: *20 min.*
COOKING TIME: *15 min.*

INGREDIENTS:
3 oz. plain flour
Pinch of salt
3 eggs
3 oz. caster sugar
Strawberry jam
¼ pint double or whipping cream
Caster or icing sugar for dusting

Butter and dust with flour and sugar two 7 in. straight-sided sandwich tins. Sift the flour with the salt twice into a bowl or on to a sheet of greaseproof paper. Place a deep mixing bowl over a pan of hot water, break the eggs into the bowl and gradually whisk in the sugar. Continue whisking until the mixture is pale, and thick enough to leave a trail. Carefully fold in the sifted flour and salt. Divide the mixture equally between the two tins, putting any scrapings from the bowl at the side of the tins, not in the middle. Bake just above the centre of an oven, pre-heated to 375°F (mark 5), for about 15 minutes or until pale brown and springy to the touch.

Carefully ease away the edges of the baked cakes with a palette knife, and cool on a wire rack.

When cold, spread the bases of both sponges with a thin layer of jam, cover one sponge with whipped cream and place the other cake, jam downwards, on top. Press lightly together and dust with caster or sifted icing sugar. Chill until serving.

Swiss Roll

PREPARATION TIME: *15 min.*
COOKING TIME: *10 min.*

INGREDIENTS:
3 oz. plain flour
Pinch of salt
3 large eggs
3 oz. caster sugar
1 tablespoon hot water
Jam or cream filling

Sift the flour and salt twice into a bowl or on to greaseproof paper. Butter a Swiss-roll tin measuring 12 in. by 8 in., and line with buttered greaseproof or non-stick paper.

Put the eggs and caster sugar in a large bowl over a pan of hot water, and whisk until the mix-

MAKING A SWISS ROLL

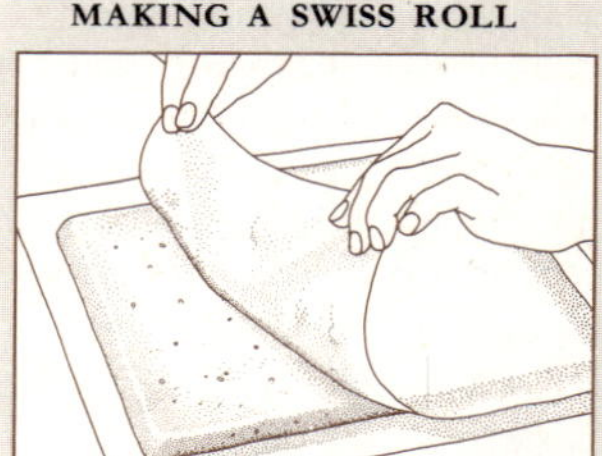

Remove lining paper from cake

Spread warm jam over cake

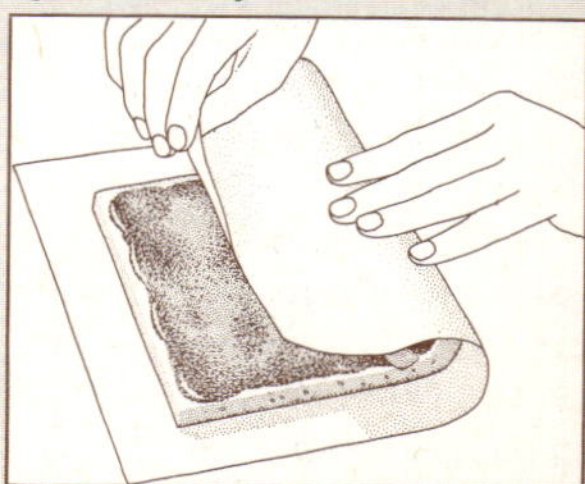

Roll up sponge on sugared paper

ture is pale and leaves a thick trail. Remove from the heat, sift half the flour and salt over the egg mixture, and fold it in carefully, using a large metal spoon. Repeat with the remaining flour, and add the hot water. Turn the mixture quickly into the prepared tin, tilting it until evenly covered with the mixture. Bake at once just above the centre of an oven, pre-heated to 425°F (mark 7), for about 10 minutes or until well-risen, light golden and springy.

Have ready a sheet of sugar-dredged greaseproof or non-stick paper. Turn the soft cake out on to the paper at once, remove the lining paper and quickly trim off the crisp edges from the sponge with a sharp knife. Spread with 4–5 tablespoons warm jam, to within ½ in. of the edges. Roll up the sponge at once from the short side, making the first turn firm, then rolling it lightly. Cool on a wire rack covered with a clean tea towel, and with the join of the sponge underneath.

The Swiss roll may also be spread with a butter-cream filling, just before serving. In this case, do not remove the lining paper, but roll the sponge round it while still warm. When cold, carefully unroll the sponge, then spread with whipped cream, butter cream, or pastry cream and roll up again.

Before serving, dust with caster or sifted icing sugar.

MELTED CAKES

These have a dense, slightly tacky texture and a consistency similar to a thick batter. Treacle or syrup is a major ingredient, with baking powder as the main raising agent together with bicarbonate of soda.

Gingerbread

PREPARATION TIME: *15 min.*
COOKING TIME: *1½ hours*

INGREDIENTS:
1 lb. plain flour
3 level teaspoons ground ginger
3 level teaspoons baking powder
1 level teaspoon bicarbonate of soda
1 level teaspoon salt
8 oz. Demerara sugar
6 oz. butter
6 oz. black treacle
6 oz. golden syrup
½ pint milk
1 large egg

Grease a 9 in. square cake tin, about 2 in. deep, and line with buttered greaseproof paper. Sift all the dry ingredients, except the sugar, into a large bowl. Warm the sugar, butter, treacle and syrup in a pan over low heat until the butter has just melted. Stir the melted ingredients into the centre of the dry mix, together with the milk and beaten egg. Beat thoroughly with a wooden spoon. Pour the mixture into the prepared tin and bake in the centre of an oven, pre-heated to 350°F (mark 4), for about 1½ hours, or until well-risen and just firm to the touch.

Cool in the tin for 15 minutes, then turn out on a wire rack. When cold, wrap in foil, without removing lining paper, and store for 4–7 days to give flavour time to mellow.

Parkin

PREPARATION TIME: *20 min.*
COOKING TIME: *45 min.*

INGREDIENTS:
8 oz. plain flour
Pinch of salt
2 level teaspoons baking powder
2 level teaspoons ground ginger
2 oz. margarine or butter
2 oz. lard
8 oz. medium oatmeal
4 oz. caster sugar
6 oz. golden syrup
6 oz. black treacle
4 tablespoons milk

Grease a tin, 10 in. by 8 in. by 1½ in. deep and line with buttered greaseproof paper. Sift together the flour, salt, baking powder and ginger into a bowl. Cut the margarine and lard into small pieces and rub into the flour until the mixture resembles fine breadcrumbs. Stir in the oatmeal and sugar. Warm the syrup and treacle, pour it into the centre of the dry ingredients, together with the milk, and beat lightly with a wooden spoon until thoroughly blended.

Turn the mixture into the prepared tin, and bake in the centre of a pre-heated oven at 350°F (mark 4) for about 45 minutes or until the mixture has begun to shrink away from the sides of the tin. It often sinks slightly. Cool on a wire rack. Leave the lining paper in place, wrap the cake in foil and store for at least a week.

ENRICHED BUTTER SPONGE CAKES

When butter is added to a whisked sponge mixture, it is known as Genoese sponge, a richer variety than fatless sponges and one which needs slightly longer baking, but keeps better.

Genoese Sponge

PREPARATION TIME: *15 min.*
COOKING TIME: *30 min.*

INGREDIENTS:
1½ oz. unsalted butter
2½ oz. plain flour
1 level tablespoon cornflour
3 large eggs
3 oz. caster sugar

Grease a 9 in. straight-sided sandwich tin, a deep, 8 in. cake tin, or a 7 in. square tin, and line with buttered greaseproof paper. Heat the butter in a pan over low heat until melted but not hot; remove from the heat and leave to stand for a few minutes. Sift together the flour and cornflour three times. Put the eggs in a large deep bowl over a pan of hot water, whisk for a few seconds, then add the sugar and continue whisking until the mixture is quite pale in colour and leaves a thick trail when the whisk is lifted out.

Remove the bowl from the heat and whisk for a few minutes longer, until the mixture is cool. Using a metal spoon, carefully fold in half the sifted flour, then pour in the melted butter in a thin stream at the side of the bowl. Fold in the remaining sifted flour. Turn this mixture into the prepared tin and bake near the top of an oven, pre-heated to 375°F (mark 5), for about 30 minutes or until well-risen and spongy to the touch. Invert on to a wire rack and leave to cool; remove lining paper.

The sponge, if baked in a deep tin, can be split horizontally into three equal layers and sandwiched together with a cream and fruit or butter cream filling, and the top decorated with cream. A shallower sponge should be split into two layers only.

A sponge baked in a large shallow tin can be cut into fancy individual shapes. Brush these with warm apricot glaze and cover with plain or coloured glacé or fondant icing. Decorate with glacé cherries, etc.

Cake fillings and toppings/ 1

Butter cream

Cooked fudge frosting

Fluffy cooked frosting

Soft sugar icing

Using fillings and toppings

Fillings and toppings serve not only to make a cake more attractive, they also have a practical use. Cakes which have been filled and iced stay moist longer. There are four basic types of fillings: butter cream, cooked fudge frosting, fluffy cooked frosting and soft sugar icing. For some of these, a sugar thermometer is essential.

Butter Cream

This is perhaps the most frequently used filling and topping. The sugar, which may be caster or icing sugar or a mixture of both, is added in small amounts to creamed butter, then beaten to a light spreading consistency. Whole eggs, egg whites or yolks may also be added.

Cooked Fudge Frosting

This needs careful attention, as the soft fudge sets quickly and makes spreading difficult. It is used as a topping rather than a filling. A sugar mixture is cooked to a given temperature, cooled, then beaten until creamy. If the frosting sets too quickly, the bowl can be placed over hot water and a teaspoon or two of warm water or milk beaten in.

Fluffy Cooked Frosting

For this type of frosting, sugar, egg whites, water and flavourings are beaten over boiling water until the mixture stands in stiff peaks. A similar frosting can be made by cooking a syrup from sugar and water, then beating it slowly into whisked egg whites. Both types of frosting spread and swirl easily, but they develop a thin sugar crust after a few days.

Soft Sugar Icing

This is an uncooked icing comprised of icing sugar and a liquid, together with flavouring and colouring. All soft icings are easy to use and go well with soft-textured cakes such as sponges. The icing coats the surface smoothly; it is poured over the cake and left to find its own level. A Royal icing used for wedding and birthday cakes is a cross between a fluffy cooked frosting and a soft sugar icing.

Using Fillings and Toppings

Numerous variations are possible with a little flair and imagination, but the basic procedure should always be followed:

Always cool a cake thoroughly before filling and icing, and brush off any loose crumbs which would stick to the icing.

Cut surfaces, such as those produced when a slab cake is cut up into smaller cakes, are often covered with a thin layer of almond glacé or fondant icing.

Do not put a firm-textured frosting or filling on a soft crumbly surface. For crumbly sponge cakes, use a light cream filling which spreads easily.

Make sure that the top of the cake is completely flat if it is to be iced. The cake can be turned upside down and the underside iced if this is more level.

To sandwich two layers of cake, place one layer, top side down, on a plate or flat surface and spread the filling to the edge. Allow the filling to set for a few minutes, then place the second layer, top side up, on the filling and lightly press the two together.

Before coating a cake with soft icing, put the cake on a wire rack over a plate. Pour the icing over the centre of the plain or filled cake, and gradually work the icing over the top and down the sides with a palette knife.

For a professional touch, spread the icing evenly round the sides of the cake before rolling it in chopped nuts or chocolate vermicelli. Spread the icing evenly over the top of the cake, then pipe on coloured icing in thin lines, $\frac{1}{2}$–$\frac{3}{4}$ in. apart, using a plain writing tube. Before the icing has set, draw lines, at right angles, over the coloured icing with the blunt edge of a knife blade. Turn the cake 180 degrees and draw the knife between the intersections.

To coat a cake with butter cream, place it on a board and decorate the sides first. Spread the coating evenly round the sides, using a round-bladed knife, then pile more butter cream on top of the cake. Smooth the cream evenly to the edges with a small palette knife, then finish the top with a swirled, latticed or roughed up pattern, using a fork, knife or confectioner's comb.

The sides may also be covered with butter cream and then decorated. Cover the sides before the top, spreading the cream evenly with a palette knife. Roll the sides carefully in chocolate vermicelli or chopped nuts, then spread butter cream or fondant icing over the top.

Piped decorations should be applied after the covering icing has set, but shaped decorations, such as rose buds, should be applied while the icing is still soft.

To make rose buds from coloured Royal icing, fix a small square of waxed paper to an icing nail with a little of the soft icing. Using a plain or star-shaped small nozzle on the icing bag, pipe a centre cone on to the paper, and then pipe on small petal shapes. Work from right to left and overlap the petals slightly until a rose of the required size is formed. Remove the waxed paper, and when the rose bud has set place it on the still soft icing.

FEATHERED GLACÉ ICING

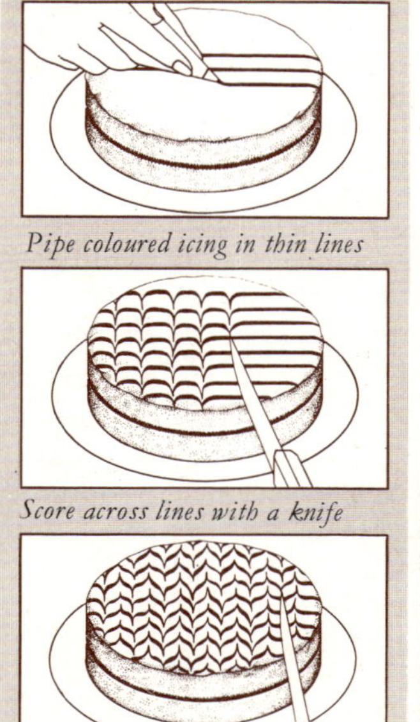

Pipe coloured icing in thin lines

Score across lines with a knife

Turn cake and score again

ROYAL ICING ROSES

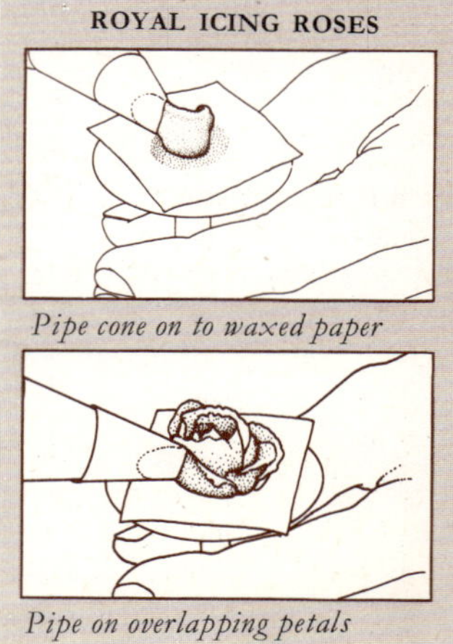

Pipe cone on to waxed paper

Pipe on overlapping petals

Cake fillings and toppings/ 2

Butter cream

Rich butter cream

Honey butter frosting

Caramel icing

Chocolate fudge frosting

American frosting

Seven-minute frosting

Butter Cream

PREPARATION TIME: *10 min.*

INGREDIENTS:

4 oz. butter or margarine
6–8 oz. icing sugar
Vanilla essence (optional)
1–2 tablespoons milk

Beat the softened butter with a wooden spoon or in an electric mixer, until creamy. Gradually beat in the sifted icing sugar a spoonful at a time, adding a few drops of vanilla essence (if used) and the milk for a more liquid consistency. This amount is sufficient to coat the sides and top of a 7 in. cake.

To this basic butter cream, a number of different flavours may be added:

Almond: add 2 level tablespoons finely chopped, toasted almonds. Substitute almond essence for vanilla essence.

Chocolate: add 1–1½ oz. melted chocolate and omit 1 tablespoon milk; alternatively, blend 1 level tablespoon cocoa with 1 tablespoon hot water, cool and add omitting the milk.

Coffee: omit vanilla essence and milk; flavour with 2 level teaspoons instant coffee blended with 1 teaspoon water, or use 2–3 teaspoons coffee essence.

Ginger: omit vanilla essence; add 2 oz. finely chopped stem ginger.

Liqueur: omit milk and vanilla essence; add 2–3 teaspoons liqueur.

Mocca: omit vanilla essence, mix 2 level teaspoons cocoa with 2 level teaspoons instant coffee powder to a smooth paste with hot water, cool before adding and omit milk.

Orange: omit vanilla essence and milk; beat in 2 tablespoons fresh orange juice, the finely grated rind of 1 small orange and, if wanted, 1 teaspoon orange bitters.

Rich Butter Cream (Crème au beurre)

PREPARATION TIME: *20 min.*

INGREDIENTS:

3 oz. caster sugar
4 tablespoons water
2 egg yolks
4–6 oz. unsalted butter

Put the sugar and water in a heavy-based pan and dissolve over low heat without boiling. When dissolved, bring the syrup to the boil and boil steadily for 2–3 minutes until 225°F is reached. Beat the egg yolks in a deep bowl and pour over the syrup in a thin steady stream, whisking all the time. Continue to whisk until the mixture is thick and cool (the bowl may be stood in iced water). Cream the butter with a wooden spoon. Gradually beat the egg syrup into the butter, a little at a time.

For additional flavour, add 2 oz. plain chocolate, melted and cool but still liquid, 1–2 tablespoons coffee essence, or grated orange or lemon rind.

Honey Butter Frosting

PREPARATION TIME: *15 min.*

INGREDIENTS:

3 oz. butter
6 oz. icing sugar
1 level tablespoon clear honey
1 tablespoon lemon juice

Beat the butter, which should be at room temperature, until soft but not oily. Gradually sift in the icing sugar, beating well. Halfway through, beat in the honey and lemon juice.

Caramel Icing

PREPARATION TIME: *20 min.*

INGREDIENTS:

5 tablespoons top of the milk
3 oz. butter
2 level tablespoons caster sugar
12 oz. icing sugar

Warm the milk and butter in a small saucepan. In another pan, heat the caster sugar over a medium heat until it turns to a golden caramel. Remove both pans from the heat, pour the milk mixture over the caramel, and return to low heat. Continue heating until the caramel has dissolved, stirring occasionally. Gradually stir in the sifted icing sugar, and beat until the icing is smooth and of a spreading consistency. Use fairly quickly.

Chocolate Fudge Frosting

PREPARATION TIME: *30 min.*

INGREDIENTS:

1 lb. caster sugar
½ pint water
2 level tablespoons golden syrup
2 oz. unsalted butter
2 oz. cocoa

Place all the ingredients in a saucepan and cook, without boiling, until the sugar has dissolved. Bring to the boil and continue boiling over low heat until the sugar thermometer registers 238°F.

To prevent sticking, move the thermometer occasionally and draw a wooden spoon across the base of the pan, but do not beat. Remove the pan from the heat and leave the mixture until cool, then beat with a wooden spoon until thick. Coat the cake quickly.

American Frosting

PREPARATION TIME: *30 min.*

INGREDIENTS:

1 lb. caster or lump sugar
Pinch cream of tartar
2 egg whites
Vanilla essence (optional)

A sugar-boiling thermometer is necessary for this frosting; if this is not available, make the slightly softer Seven-Minute Frosting. Put the sugar and 8 tablespoons of water in a heavy-based pan over low heat and dissolve the sugar without stirring. Blend the cream of tartar with 1 teaspoon of water and add this paste to the syrup. Bring to the boil and continue boiling, without stirring, until the thermometer registers 240°F (read the thermometer at eye level). Just before this temperature is reached, whisk the egg whites in a large bowl until stiff. Remove the syrup from the heat and when the bubbles subside, pour the hot syrup in a long, thin stream on to the egg whites, whisking all the time. Continue whisking until the frosting is thick and opaque. Add a few drops of vanilla essence and spread the frosting quickly over an 8 in. cake.

Seven-minute Frosting

PREPARATION TIME: *10 min.*

INGREDIENTS:

1 egg white
6 oz. caster sugar
Pinch of salt
2 tablespoons water
Pinch of cream of tartar

Put all the ingredients in a deep bowl and using a rotary or electric mixer whisk for a few minutes. Place the bowl over a pan of hot water and continue to whisk until the mixture is thick enough to stand in 'peaks', after 7 minutes. Use at once in the same way as American frosting.

Cake fillings and toppings/3

Glacé icing

Fondant icing

Royal icing

Apricot glaze

Uncooked almond paste

Cooked almond paste

Glacé Icing

PREPARATION TIME: *10 min.*

INGREDIENTS:
4–6 oz. icing sugar
1–2 tablespoons warm water
Food colouring (optional)

Sift the icing sugar into a deep bowl. Add the water, a little at a time, until the mixture is thick enough to coat the back of a wooden spoon. Add a few drops of colouring if required.

A more glossy icing can be obtained by dissolving 1 oz. caster sugar in 4 tablespoons of water in a small pan over low heat. Bring to the boil and bubble gently for 5–7 minutes or until the liquid has reduced by about half. Remove the pan from the heat and cool the pan in cold water until the base is lukewarm. Beat in the sifted icing sugar, a little at a time. Use the icing at once, to cover the top of a 7 in. cake or 12–18 buns.

The basic glacé icing may be flavoured with, for example, 1 tablespoon of lemon juice to replace 1 tablespoon water, 1–1½ teaspoons coffee essence as part of the amount of water. Strained orange juice may replace all the water and a few drops of orange colouring may also be added. Alternatively, blend 2 level teaspoons of cocoa with 1 tablespoon of the water, or replace 1 tablespoon water with 1 tablespoon liqueur.

Fondant Icing

This traditional icing for petits fours is less brittle than glacé icing. It is only worthwhile making in large amounts.

PREPARATION TIME: *30 min.*

INGREDIENTS:
¼ pint water
1 lb. caster or lump sugar
Pinch of cream of tartar or 1 oz. glucose

Put the water in a large heavy-based pan, add the sugar and dissolve to a syrup, without boiling, over low heat. Using a brush dipped in cold water, wipe round the pan at the level of the syrup to prevent crystals from forming. Add the cream of tartar or glucose dissolved in a little water. Bring the syrup to the boil and continue boiling steadily until the syrup registers 240°F (read the thermometer at eye level). Pour the syrup very slowly into a heat-resistant bowl; leave until a skin forms on top.

Using a wooden spatula work the icing in a figure-of-eight movement until it becomes opaque and firm. Knead the icing until smooth and store in an airtight tin until required. Before using, heat the fondant icing in a bowl over hot water, adding a little sugar syrup until the icing has the consistency of double cream. Add flavouring and colouring as for glacé icing and use to cover about 24 petits fours or a 7–8 in. cake.

Royal Icing

PREPARATION TIME: *15 min.*

INGREDIENTS:
4 egg whites
1¾–2 lb. icing sugar
1 tablespoon lemon juice
2 teaspoons glycerine

Whisk the egg whites in a large bowl until frothy. Stir in the sifted icing sugar, a little at a time, beating thoroughly with a wooden spoon. When half the sugar has been added, beat in the lemon juice. Continue adding more sugar, beating well after each addition until the icing forms soft peaks when pulled up with a wooden spoon. For piping purposes the icing should be slightly firmer. Stir in the glycerine, which keeps the icing soft.

Ideally, leave the icing to rest for 24 hours, covered with polythene, and work it through before using. The above amount is sufficient to coat the top and sides of a 10 in. wide and 2 in. deep cake. Leave the coating to set before piping on the decorations.

An electric mixer may be used, but care must be taken not to overbeat the icing – a fluffy Royal icing results in a rough surface and will also break when piped.

Apricot Glaze

PREPARATION TIME: *15 min.*

INGREDIENTS:
1 lb. apricot jam
1 tablespoon lemon juice
4 tablespoons water

Bring all the ingredients slowly to the boil, reduce the heat and simmer for 5 minutes. Put the mixture through a sieve, return it to the pan and boil gently for another 5 minutes. Cool the apricot glaze before storing it in a screw-top jar. Use as required to glaze fruit tarts or to hold almond paste on cakes.

Uncooked Almond Paste

PREPARATION TIME: *10 min.*

INGREDIENTS:
4 oz. icing sugar
4 oz. caster sugar
8 oz. ground almonds
1 teaspoon lemon juice
Almond essence
1 egg

Sift the icing sugar into a bowl and mix in the caster sugar and almonds. Add the lemon juice and a few drops of almond essence. Gradually stir in the beaten egg using a wooden spoon or the fingers until the mixture is a firm but manageable dough. Knead lightly, and roll out.

This quantity makes enough paste to cover a 7 in. cake.

Cooked Almond Paste

This paste resembles marzipan in texture and can be used for confectionery as well as for coating.

PREPARATION TIME: *40 min.*

INGREDIENTS:
1 lb. lump sugar
¼ pint water
¼ level teaspoon cream of tartar
12 oz. ground almonds
2 egg whites
2 oz. icing sugar
Almond essence (optional)

Dissolve the lump sugar in the water over low heat. Increase the heat and bring the syrup to the boil; stir in the cream of tartar dissolved in a teaspoon of water. Boil until the syrup reaches 240°F (read the thermometer at eye level). Remove the pan from the heat and stir rapidly with a wooden spoon until the syrup becomes cloudy. Stir in the ground almonds and the unbeaten egg whites at once; return the pan to the heat for a few minutes, stirring continuously.

Turn the almond mixture on to a working surface and gradually work in the sifted icing sugar with a palette knife. As soon as the paste is cool enough, knead it with the fingers until it has a malleable consistency; add more sifted sugar if needed. Roll out the paste and use to cover a 9 in. wide cake.

When bread was home-baked, the dough which was left from the weekly bake was enriched with spices and dried fruit and became lardy cake, a baking-day treat. Yeast cakes are light, with a rich flavour, and like bread need 'strong', high-gluten flour.

Yeast cakes/1

Danish pastries

Lardy cake

Danish Pastries

PREPARATION TIME: *45 min. (plus rising)*
RESTING TIME: *50 min.*
COOKING TIME: *10 min.*

INGREDIENTS:
8 oz. plain flour
Pinch salt
1 oz. lard
1 level tablespoon caster sugar
½ oz. fresh yeast
5 tablespoons cold water
2 eggs
5 oz. unsalted butter
FILLINGS:
Almond paste
1 oz. butter
1 oz. caster sugar
1 level teaspoon cinnamon
Currants and chopped mixed peel
GARNISH:
Glacé icing

Sift the flour and salt into a large bowl. Cut up the lard and rub it into the flour with the fingertips; add the sugar and make a well in the centre of the flour. Blend the yeast with the water in a small bowl until creamy and smooth, then add it to the flour together with 1 lightly beaten egg. Gradually work in the flour, then beat the soft dough until it leaves the sides of the bowl clean.

Turn the dough out on to a lightly floured surface and knead it until smooth. Put it inside a lightly oiled polythene bag and chill for 10 minutes.

Beat the butter with a wooden spoon until soft but not oily, then shape it into a rectangle about 5 in. by 9½ in. On a floured board, roll out the dough to a 10–11 in. square and place the butter in the centre. Fold the two unbuttered sides over so that they just overlap the butter. Seal the open sides with the rolling pin, then roll the dough into an oblong strip, about three times as long as it is wide; fold in three.

Place the dough in a lightly oiled polythene bag and leave in the refrigerator for 10 minutes. Remove the polythene and roll out the dough, in the opposite direction, to an oblong strip and fold in three. Repeat the resting, rolling and folding twice more. Finally, rest the dough for 10 minutes in the refrigerator before rolling it out to any of the traditional shapes.

Almond Squares Roll out half the dough to a 10 in. square, then cut it into four equal pieces. Fold two corners of each square to meet in the centre, envelope style, and repeat with the other two corners. Press down firmly to seal. Place a small round of almond paste in the centre.

Crescents Roll out the dough as for almond squares, and cut each square diagonally in half. Place a small piece of almond paste at the base of each triangle, then roll it up from the base and curve into a crescent shape.

Pinwheels Roll out half a portion of pastry dough to a rectangle 12 in. by 8 in. Cream the butter with the sugar and cinnamon and spread over the dough to within ¼ in. of the edges. Scatter a few currants and a little mixed peel over the butter. Cut the dough in half, lengthways, and roll each piece, from the shorter end, into a thick roll. Cut this into 1 in. thick slices.

Alternatively, make cuts, 1 in. apart, through three-quarters of the depth of the rolls. Ease the near-cut pinwheels apart so that they overlap each other slightly; bake for about 30 minutes.

Set the pastry shapes well apart on greased baking trays and cover with sheets of oiled polythene. Leave the pastries to rise in a warm place for 20 minutes. Remove the polythene and brush the pastries with lightly beaten egg. Bake near the top of a pre-heated oven, at 425°F (mark 7), for about 10 minutes or until golden. Leave on a wire rack and, while still warm, brush almond squares, crescents and pinwheels with glacé icing. Leave to set before serving.

DANISH PASTRIES

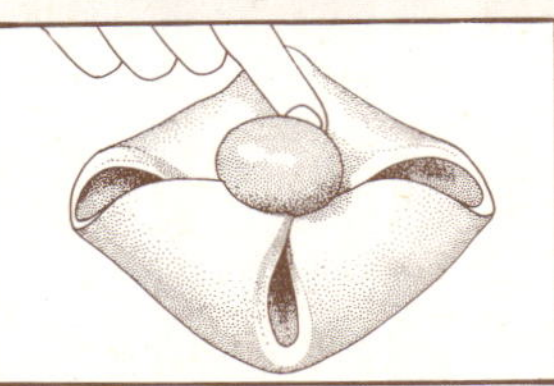
Almond square

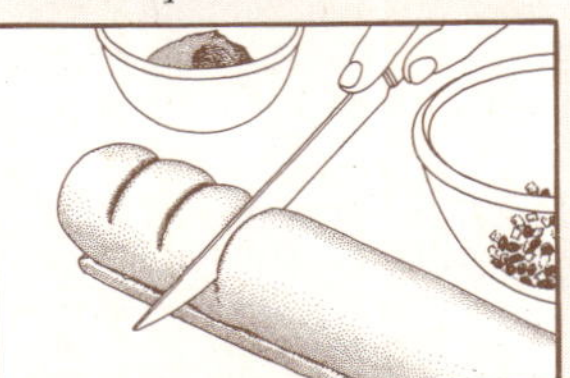
Cutting pinwheels nearly through

Overlapping pinwheels

Lardy Cake

PREPARATION TIME: *30 min. (plus rising and proving)*
COOKING TIME: *30 min.*

INGREDIENTS:
One-third portion white bread dough
4 oz. lard or margarine
4 oz. caster sugar
1 level teaspoon mixed spice
3 oz. sultanas
Cooking oil

Roll out the risen dough with a rolling pin, on a lightly floured surface, to a strip ¼ in. thick. Cut the lard into flakes and put one-third of these over the dough to within ½ in. of the edges. Mix the sugar with the spice and sultanas and sprinkle one-third over the fat. Fold the dough up loosely from one of the short sides.

Roll the dough out again into a strip and cover with another third of lard and half the remaining sugar, spice and sultanas. Roll up again, then roll out into a strip for the third time. Cover the dough with the remaining lard, sugar and sultanas.

Roll up the dough, then roll out and shape it to fit a greased roasting tin, 10 in. long by 8 in. wide. Lift the dough into the tin and press it down well, particularly in the corners. Put the tin in an oiled polythene bag and leave to rise (or prove) until doubled in size. Remove the polythene, brush the top of the dough lightly with oil and sprinkle with a little extra sugar. Score a criss-cross pattern across the surface of the dough with the point of a knife.

Bake the lardy cake in the centre, or just above, of a pre-

Yeast cakes/2

Brioches

Croissants

PREPARING A LARDY CAKE

1. *Sprinkle spiced sultanas over dough*

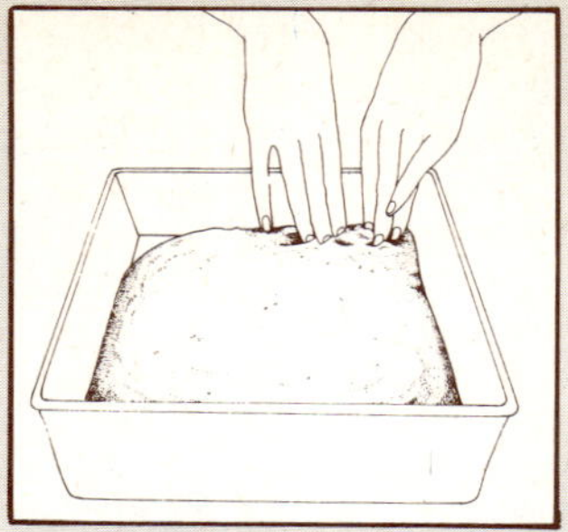
2. *Fold the dough loosely*

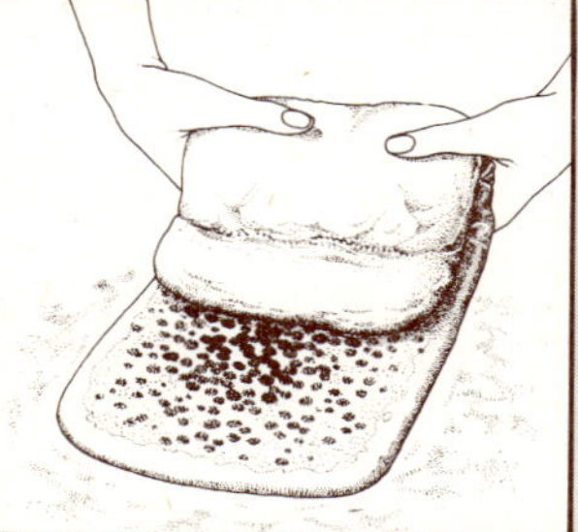
3. *Press dough into corners of tin*

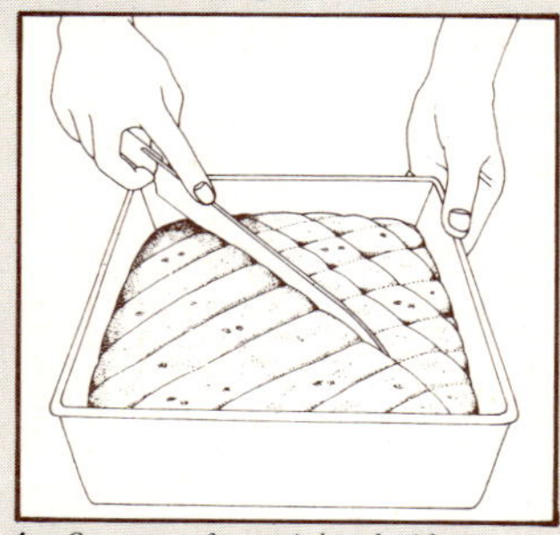
4. *Score surface with a knife*

heated oven at 425°F (mark 7) for 30 minutes. Turn the cake out of the tin and leave to cool on a wire rack. Serve lardy cake sliced, plain or buttered.

Brioches

PREPARATION TIME: *25 min. (plus rising and proving)*
COOKING TIME: *10 min.*

INGREDIENTS *(for 12 brioches):*
8 oz. strong plain flour
½ level teaspoon salt
1 level tablespoon caster sugar
½ oz. fresh yeast
1½ tablespoons warm water
2 eggs
2 oz. butter, melted

Sift the flour and salt into a bowl and add the sugar. Cream the yeast with the water in a small bowl, and stir it, together with the beaten eggs and the melted butter, into the flour with a wooden spoon. Beat the dough until it leaves the sides of the bowl clean, then turn it out on to a lightly floured surface and knead for 5 minutes.

Put the dough in an oiled polythene bag and leave it to rise at room temperature for 1–1½ hours or until it has doubled in size. Turn the risen dough on to a lightly floured surface and knead it until smooth. Shape the dough into a sausage and divide it into 12 equal pieces.

Brush 3 in. fluted patty pans with oil and shape three-quarters of each piece of dough into a ball; place it in a patty pan. Using a floured finger, press a hole in the centre of the dough as far as the base of the tin. Shape the remaining piece of dough into a knob and insert it in the hole. Press lightly with the fingertip to unite the two pieces of dough. When all 12 brioches have been shaped, set the patty pans on a baking tray and cover them with oiled polythene. Leave to rise (prove) until the dough is puffy and just below the tops of the tins.

BRIOCHES

Brush fluted tins with oil

Insert dough knob in centre

Remove the polythene and bake the brioches in the centre of a pre-heated oven at 450°F (mark 8) for 10 minutes or until golden brown.

Croissants

PREPARATION TIME: *1–1½ hours (plus rising and proving)*
RESTING TIME: *1 hour*
COOKING TIME: *15–20 min.*

INGREDIENTS *(for 12 croissants):*
1 lb. strong plain flour
2 level teaspoons salt
1 oz. lard
1 oz. fresh yeast
½ pint warm water, less 4 tablespoons
2 eggs
4–6 oz. hard margarine or butter
½ level teaspoon caster sugar

Sift the flour and salt into a bowl. Cut up the lard and rub this into the flour with the fingertips until blended to a coarse breadcrumb consistency. Cream the yeast with the water in a small bowl and pour it into a well in the centre of the flour, together with one lightly beaten egg. Gradually incorporate the flour with one hand and beat the dough until it leaves the sides of the bowl clean.

Transfer the dough to a lightly floured surface and knead it for about 10 minutes, until smooth. Roll out the dough to a strip, about 20 in. by 8 in. and ¼ in. thick. If necessary, trim the edges with a knife. Soften the margarine with a knife until pliable but not creamy, and divide it into three portions. Flake one portion of the margarine and dot it over the upper two-thirds of the dough, leaving a ½ in. border round the edges.

Fold the dough into three, bringing up first the unbuttered part of the dough, then folding the opposite part over. Give the dough a half turn, and seal the edges by pressing with the rolling pin. Shape into a long strip again by gently pressing the dough at intervals with the rolling pin, and roll out to a rectangle. Dot as before with the second portion of flaked margarine, then fold, turn the pastry and roll again before adding the last of the margarine. Fold in three again.

MAKING CROISSANTS

Flake fat over two-thirds of dough

Fold the dough into three

Seal with a rolling pin

Roll up dough triangles

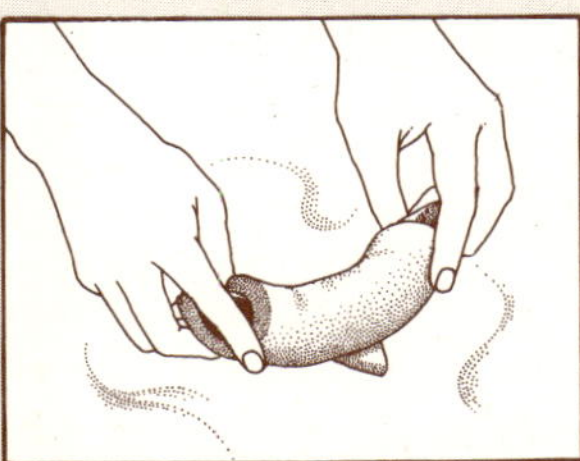
Curve pastry to a crescent

Work as quickly as possible to avoid the dough becoming warm and soft, thus melting the margarine. Keep the edges straight and the corners square.

Put the folded dough in an oiled polythene bag and leave in the refrigerator for 30 minutes. Remove the polythene, roll out the dough and repeat the rolling and folding three times more, but without adding any fat. Return to the oiled polythene bag and the refrigerator for another 30 minutes.

To shape the croissants, roll the dough out, on a lightly floured surface, to a rectangle about 22 in. by 13 in. Cover with oiled polythene and leave on the table for 10 minutes. Trim the edges with a sharp knife, to a rectangle 21 in. by 12 in.; divide the dough in half lengthways. Cut each strip into six triangles, 6 in. wide at the base.

Beat one egg with a few drops of water and the sugar, and brush over the triangles. Roll up each triangle loosely, finishing with the tip underneath, then carefully curve the pastry into a crescent shape. Place the croissants, well spaced, on ungreased baking trays.

Brush the tops with a little more egg glaze, cover them with oiled polythene and leave at room temperature to rise (prove) for about 30 minutes or until light and puffy. Brush again with egg glaze before baking the croissants in the centre of a pre-heated oven at 425°F (mark 7) for 15–20 minutes. Use a palette knife to ease the croissants off the baking tray, and serve them while still warm.

Chelsea Buns

PREPARATION TIME: *20 min. (plus rising and proving)*
COOKING TIME: *30–35 min.*

INGREDIENTS *(for 9 buns):*
8 oz. strong plain flour
½ level teaspoon caster sugar
½ oz. fresh yeast
4 fluid oz. warm (110°F) milk
½ level teaspoon salt
½ oz. margarine or lard
1 egg
3 oz. dried fruit (sultanas, currants or seedless raisins)
1 oz. chopped mixed peel
2 oz. light soft brown sugar
½–1 oz. melted butter
Clear honey

Sift 2 oz. of the measured flour into a bowl and add the caster sugar. Crumble in the yeast and beat in the milk with a wooden spoon. Leave this yeast mixture in a warm place for about 20 minutes or until frothy. Sift together the remaining flour and the salt and rub in the margarine. Make a well in the centre, add the beaten egg and pour in the yeast mixture. Using one hand, gradually work in the flour.

Beat the dough in the bowl until it leaves the sides clean; it should be fairly soft and pliable. Turn the dough on to a lightly floured surface and knead it for 10 minutes, until smooth. Put it in a lightly oiled polythene bag and leave it to rise at room temperature for 1–1½ hours or until it has doubled in size.

Knead the risen dough on a lightly floured surface until smooth, then roll it out with a well-floured rolling pin, to a rectangle 12 in. by 9 in. Mix the dried fruit, peel and soft brown sugar together, brush the dough with melted butter and spread the fruit mixture on top to within ½ in. along the longer edges. Roll up the dough from the long sides and press the join to seal it.

Cut the roll into nine equal slices and lay them flat, in rows of three, in a greased, 7 in. square cake tin. Leave to rise in a polythene bag, in a warm place, for about 30 minutes.

Remove the polythene bag and bake the buns in the centre of a pre-heated oven at 375°F (mark 5) for 30–35 minutes. Turn the buns on to a wire rack and, while still hot, brush them with honey.

CHELSEA BUNS

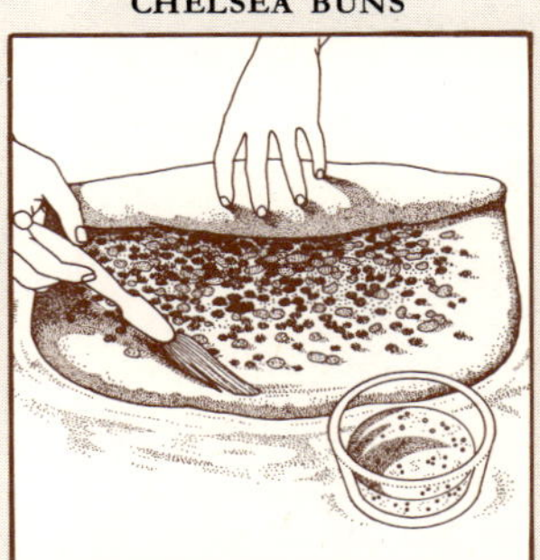
Roll dough like Swiss Roll

Cut roll into slices

Biscuits/1

The word 'biscuit' comes from the French *bis cuit*, 'twice cooked', and this is a literal description of what happened in the early days of biscuit-making. At the start of a long sea voyage, small, hard cakes were taken aboard, to form part of the crew's daily diet. These cakes had to be cooked before loading, otherwise they would have gone mouldy, and before eating their 'hard tack', the sailors would have the cakes cooked again. Biscuits today are only once cooked, and although usually at their best when freshly baked, some can be stored in airtight containers for about 1 week.

Bake biscuits at or just above the centre of the oven; if two baking trays are used place them above each other in the oven, and halfway through baking switch them over so that all the biscuits brown evenly. Cool the baked biscuits on a wire rack, lifting them from the baking trays as soon as cooked. Some biscuits, however, especially those made with syrup or honey, are soft when baking is completed – leave these on the trays to settle for a few minutes.

Generally, biscuits fall into one of half a dozen main groups: bar types, drop cookies, shaped cookies, piped cookies, prepared biscuits and rolled biscuits.

SHAPED COOKIES

The dough for shaped cookies is fairly soft and needs quick and light handling. Alternatively, it can be chilled in the refrigerator until stiff, and moulded in the palms of the hands.

Ginger Nuts

PREPARATION TIME: *15 min.*
COOKING TIME: *15 min.*

INGREDIENTS *(for 24 biscuits)*.
4 oz. self-raising flour
½ level teaspoon bicarbonate of soda
1 level teaspoon ground ginger
½ level teaspoon ground cinnamon
2 level teaspoons caster sugar
2 oz. butter
3 oz. golden syrup

Grease two or three baking trays. Sift the flour, bicarbonate of soda, ginger and cinnamon into a bowl; add the sugar. In a small pan, melt the butter, without boiling, and stir in the syrup. Mix this into the dry ingredients, using a wooden spoon. Shape the dough between the hands into a thick sausage shape before cutting it into 24 even pieces. Roll each piece into a small ball, set them well apart on the baking trays and flatten slightly.

Bake just above the centre of an oven pre-heated to 375°F (mark 5) for about 15 minutes, or until the tops have cracked and are golden brown. Cool for a few minutes on the baking tray before lifting on to a wire rack. As soon as quite cold, store ginger nuts in an airtight tin, as they quickly go soft.

Jumbles

PREPARATION TIME: *40 min.*
COOKING TIME: *12–15 min.*

INGREDIENTS *(for 10–15 biscuits)*:
2½ oz. butter
2½ oz. caster sugar
Half a beaten egg
5 oz. self-raising flour
1 teaspoon finely grated lemon rind
1 oz. ground almonds

Grease two baking trays. Cream the butter with a wooden spoon until soft, but not oily, then add the sugar and continue beating until light and fluffy. Beat in the egg and add the sifted flour, lemon rind and almonds. Form the mixture into three rolls, ½–¾ in. wide; cut these into 4 in. long pieces and form them into 'S' shapes.

Place on the baking trays, and bake in the centre of a pre-heated oven at 400°F (mark 6) for about 12 minutes, or until risen and pale brown. Cool for a few minutes, then transfer to a wire rack.

Orange Creams

PREPARATION TIME: *30 min.*
COOKING TIME: *20 min.*

INGREDIENTS *(for 18 biscuits)*:
4 oz. butter
3–4 oz. caster sugar
2 level teaspoons golden syrup
1 egg yolk
Finely grated rind of an orange
7 oz. plain flour
½ level teaspoon cream of tartar
1 level teaspoon baking powder
FILLING:
2 oz. butter
3 oz. icing sugar
Orange juice

Grease two or three baking trays. Cream the butter and sugar, using a wooden spoon, until light and fluffy. Beat in the syrup, egg yolk and orange rind. Sift the flour, cream of tartar and baking powder over the creamed ingredients and fold in with a metal spoon to give a soft dough.

Shape the dough into 36 balls about the size of large marbles and set them well apart on the baking sheets. Bake just above the centre of a pre-heated oven at 375°F (mark 5) for about 20 minutes, or until lightly coloured and risen. Cool on a wire rack.

For the filling, beat the butter until soft, then gradually beat in the sifted icing sugar with as much orange juice as the filling will take without becoming too soft. Colour it pale orange.

Spread the filling over half the biscuits, and sandwich together.

PIPED COOKIES

The dough for piped cookies is fairly soft and should be piped through a medium-sized fabric forcing bag often fitted with a star-shaped vegetable nozzle.

Lemon Meltaways

PREPARATION TIME: *20 min.*
RESTING TIME: *30 min.*
COOKING TIME: *30 min.*

INGREDIENTS *(for about 20 biscuits)*:
4 oz. butter or block margarine
1 oz. icing sugar
Finely grated rind of half lemon
4 oz. plain flour
Sieved apricot jam
GLAZE:
2 level tablespoons icing sugar
2 teaspoons lemon juice, approx.

Grease two baking trays. In a deep bowl, beat the butter with a wooden spoon until creamy, add the sifted icing sugar and continue beating until the mixture is pale and fluffy. Stir in the lemon rind and flour to give a soft dough. Spoon the mixture into a forcing bag, fitted with a medium star vegetable nozzle, and pipe out about 20 shell shapes, a little apart from each other. Chill for 30 minutes in the refrigerator.

Bake in the centre of a pre-heated oven at 325°F (mark 3) for about 25 minutes or until lightly browned. For the glaze, blend the sifted icing sugar with enough lemon juice to give a coating consistency.

Leave the baked biscuits on the baking trays, brush them with soft sieved jam and then with the lemon glaze. Return the biscuits to the oven for a further 5 minutes, then set them on a wire rack to cool and crisp.

Short Fingers

PREPARATION TIME: *45 min.*
COOKING TIME: *10–15 min.*

INGREDIENTS *(for 12 biscuits):*
4½ oz. butter
1 oz. icing sugar
5 oz. plain flour
3 oz. plain cooking chocolate
BUTTER CREAM:
1 oz. butter
2 oz. icing sugar
Vanilla essence

Grease two baking trays. Cream the butter with a wooden spoon until soft, but not oily, then beat in the sifted icing sugar. Stir in the sifted flour. Put the mixture in a forcing bag, fitted with a medium star vegetable nozzle, and pipe it in 2 in. long fingers, on to the baking trays. Bake just above or in the centre of a pre-heated oven, at 375°F (mark 5) for 10–15 minutes or until pale golden brown.

Meanwhile, break the chocolate into small pieces and place them in a bowl over hot water until melted. To make the butter cream, cream the butter until soft, then beat in the sifted icing sugar and a few drops of vanilla.

Leave the baked biscuits to cool completely on a wire rack. When cold, sandwich them in pairs with the butter cream. Dip one end of each biscuit in the melted chocolate and place them on a rack with the chocolate end protruding over the edge. When the chocolate has set, repeat the procedure with the other ends. Leave the biscuits for about 1½ hours before serving.

SHORT FINGERS

Pipe out 2 in. long fingers

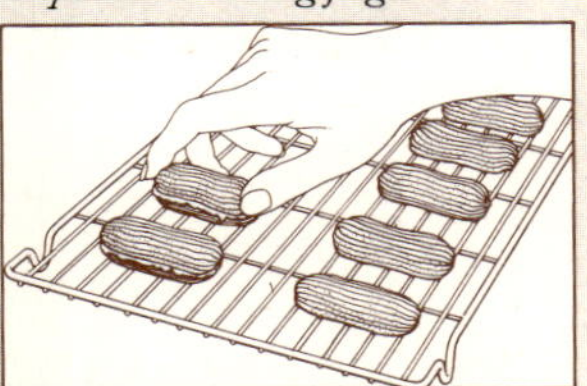

Sandwich with butter cream

Coat tips of biscuits in chocolate

Macaroons

PREPARATION TIME: *10 min.*
COOKING TIME: *15 min.*

INGREDIENTS *(for 24 biscuits):*
Rice paper
4 oz. ground almonds
6 oz. caster sugar
2 egg whites
1 level tablespoon cornflour
¼ teaspoon vanilla essence
12 blanched almonds

Line two or three baking trays with rice paper. Mix the ground almonds with the sugar and add the unbeaten egg whites, setting 1 tablespoon aside. Using a wooden spoon, work the mixture until the ingredients are evenly blended. Stir in the cornflour, vanilla essence and 2 teaspoons of water. Spoon the mixture into a forcing bag fitted with a ½ in. plain nozzle. Pipe the biscuits on to the rice paper in large round buttons; top each with half an almond. Brush lightly with the remaining egg white.

Bake the macaroons just above or in the centre of a pre-heated oven, at 375°F (mark 5), for about 15 minutes or until lightly browned, risen and slightly cracked. Cut the rice paper to fit round each macaroon and leave to cool on a wire rack. Serve preferably on the day of baking.

DROP COOKIES

Baked drop cookies can be soft with a cake-like texture, or crisp and even brittle, often irregular in shape. The soft dough is dropped in mounds on to a baking tray.

Brandy Snaps

PREPARATION TIME: *15 min.*
COOKING TIME: *20–30 min.*

INGREDIENTS *(for 16 biscuits):*
2 oz. butter
2 oz. caster sugar
2 level tablespoons golden syrup
2 oz. plain flour
½ level teaspoon ground ginger
1 teaspoon brandy
Finely grated rind of half lemon
FILLING:
6 fluid oz. double cream
1 tablespoon milk

BRANDY SNAPS

Roll snap round spoon handle

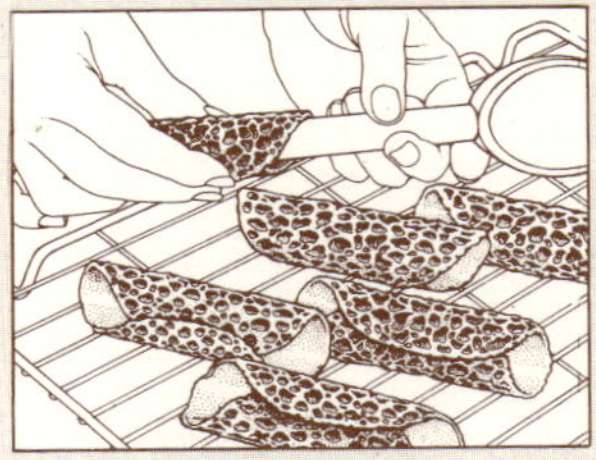

Remove shaped brandy snap

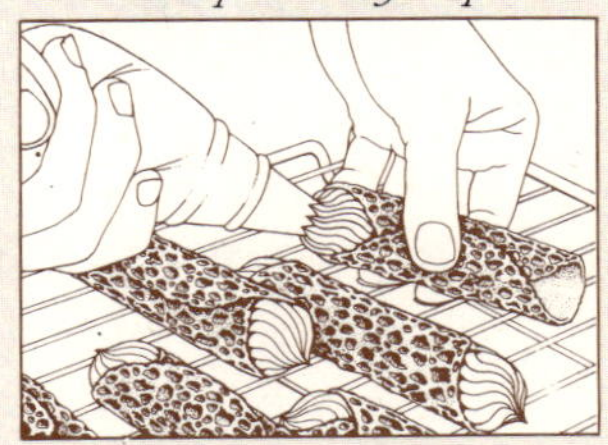

Pipe cream into brandy snaps

Grease or line two baking trays with non-stick kitchen paper, and butter the handles of a few wooden spoons thoroughly. Melt the butter, with the sugar and syrup over low heat. Stir until smooth, then remove.

Sift the flour and ginger, and stir it into the melted ingredients, together with the brandy and lemon rind. Mix thoroughly with a wooden spoon, and leave to cool for 1–2 minutes.

Drop the mixture in teaspoons, at 4 in. intervals, on to the baking trays. Bake towards the top of a pre-heated oven, at 350°F (mark 4), for 7–10 minutes or until the biscuits are bubbly, lacy in texture and golden brown. Rotate the baking so that not too many will be ready for rolling at the same time.

Biscuits/3

Coconut wafers

Ginger drops

Bar-type biscuits

Boston brownies

Shortbread

Spiced black currant bars

Remove the biscuits from the oven and quickly roll each snap loosely round a buttered spoon handle, easing them round with a palette knife. Leave the snaps on the handles until set, then twist them gently off and cool on a wire rack. If the biscuits set before they have all been shaped into snaps, return them to the oven for a few minutes until soft and pliable again.

Just before serving, whisk together the cream and milk until light and fluffy. Pipe or spoon the cream into both ends of each snap. Unfilled brandy snaps will keep in an airtight container for up to 1 week.

Coconut Wafers

PREPARATION TIME: *20 min.*
COOKING TIME: *12 min.*

INGREDIENTS *(for 18 biscuits):*
2 oz. butter
2 oz. caster sugar
1 level tablespoon golden syrup
2 teaspoons lemon juice
2 oz. plain flour
1 oz. fine desiccated coconut

Grease two or three baking trays. Cream the butter and sugar until light and fluffy, then beat in the syrup. Add the lemon juice, sifted flour and the coconut. Drop the dough in teaspoons on to the baking trays, setting them well apart as the wafers spread.

Bake just below the centre of an oven pre-heated to 350°F (mark 4) for about 12 minutes, when the edges of the wafers should be golden brown and the centres lightly coloured. Cool slightly before lifting carefully from the baking trays on to a wire rack.

Ginger Drops

PREPARATION TIME: *10 min.*
COOKING TIME: *15–20 min.*

INGREDIENTS *(for 18 biscuits):*
4 oz. plain flour
½ level teaspoon bicarbonate of soda
1 level teaspoon ground ginger
1 oz. golden syrup
1 oz. stem ginger, chopped
2 oz. butter or margarine
2 oz. Demerara sugar
2 tablespoons milk

Grease two baking trays. Sift together the flour, bicarbonate of soda and ginger. Gently melt the syrup. Cream the butter and sugar until light and fluffy, then stir in the syrup and stem ginger, half the sifted flour and 1 tablespoon of milk. Add the remaining flour and milk and mix to a soft dough. Drop the mixture in teaspoons, easing it off with the little finger, on to the baking trays, setting them well apart.

Bake just above the centre of an oven pre-heated to 350°F (mark 4) for about 15 minutes. Cool on a wire rack.

BAR-TYPE BISCUITS

These have a cake-like texture, with the exception of shortbread, and are baked in one complete piece before being cut up.

Boston Brownies

PREPARATION TIME: *15 min.*
COOKING TIME: *35 min.*

INGREDIENTS *(for 16–20 biscuits):*
2½ oz. butter or block margarine
2 oz. cooking chocolate
6 oz. caster sugar
2½ oz. self-raising flour
Pinch of salt
2 eggs
½ teaspoon vanilla essence
2 oz. shelled walnuts

Grease and flour a shallow 8 in. square tin. Melt the butter and chocolate in a bowl over hot water, and add the sugar. Sift the flour and salt into a bowl, and stir in the chocolate mixture, beaten eggs, vanilla essence and chopped walnuts. Beat the mixture until smooth, then spoon into the prepared tin.

Bake in the centre of an oven pre-heated to 350°F (mark 4) for about 35 minutes or until the mixture is risen and beginning to leave the sides of the tin. Leave in the tin to cool slightly before cutting the cake into 1½–2 in. squares.

Shortbread

PREPARATION TIME: *20 min.*
RESTING TIME: *1 hour*
COOKING TIME: *1 hour*

INGREDIENTS *(for 8 biscuits):*
5 oz. plain flour
Pinch of salt
1 oz. rice flour or ground rice
2 oz. caster sugar
4 oz. butter or block margarine

Sift the flour, salt and rice flour into a bowl. Add the sugar and grate the butter, taken straight from the refrigerator, into the dry ingredients. Work the mixture with the fingertips until it resembles breadcrumbs. Press the mixture into a 7 in. straight-sided sandwich tin and level the top. Prick the top all over with a fork and mark the mixture into eight equal portions, cutting through to the base of the tin.

Chill the shortbread in the refrigerator for 1 hour, then bake in the centre of a pre-heated oven, at 300°F (mark 2), for about 1 hour or until pale-straw coloured. Cool the shortbread in the tin before cooling it on a wire rack. Break into wedges.

SHORTBREAD

Grate butter into flour and rice

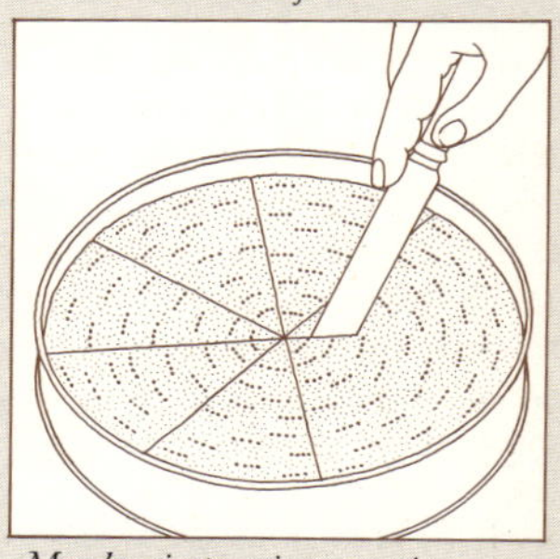
Mark mixture into portions

Spiced Black Currant Bars

PREPARATION TIME: *25 min.*
RESTING TIME: *1 hour*
COOKING TIME: *30 min.*

INGREDIENTS *(for 16 biscuits):*
8 oz. plain flour
Pinch of salt
2 level teaspoons baking powder
2 level teaspoons mixed spice
4 oz. butter or block margarine
5 oz. caster sugar
1 level tablespoon golden syrup
1 large egg, beaten
½ lb. black currant jam
3 oz. shelled walnuts

Sift together the flour, salt, baking powder and spice. Cream the butter with the sugar until light and fluffy, then beat in the syrup and beaten egg. Fold in the flour and mix the ingredients thoroughly to a manageable

SPICED BLACK CURRANT BARS

Spread jam over grated dough

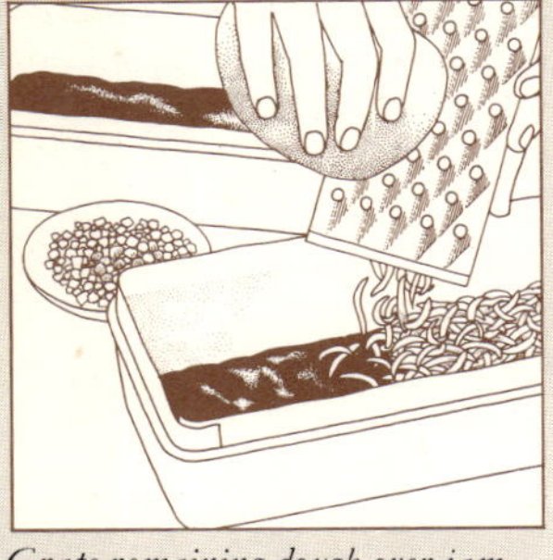

Grate remaining dough over jam

dough. Wrap this loosely in kitchen foil and chill until firm, about 1 hour.

Grease and line two shallow 12 in. by 4 in. cake tins. Coarsely grate or flake half the chilled dough into the tins, and press the top down lightly. Spread the jam over the dough, then grate the remaining dough over the jam and top with the chopped walnuts. Bake just above the centre of an oven pre-heated to 350°F (mark 4) for about 30 minutes. Leave to cool in the tins. Cut into bars, about $1\frac{1}{2}$ in. wide.

ROLLED BISCUITS

For rolled biscuits the dough must be stiff enough to be rolled to a thickness of $\frac{1}{8}$–$\frac{1}{4}$ in. before cutting out a variety of shapes. Dough that is difficult to handle, is best rolled between sheets of non-stick paper.

Butter Shorts

PREPARATION TIME: *30 min.*
COOKING TIME: *25 min.*

INGREDIENTS *(for 16 biscuits):*
4 oz. butter
2 oz. caster sugar
6 oz. plain flour
Caster sugar for dredging

Grease two baking trays. Cream the butter with a wooden spoon until soft, but not oily, add the sugar and beat until pale and fluffy. Work in the sifted flour and knead lightly together with the fingertips to form a ball. Roll this out $\frac{1}{8}$ in. thick, on a lightly floured surface or between sheets of non-stick paper.

Using a $2\frac{1}{2}$–$2\frac{3}{4}$ in. fluted pastry cutter, stamp out rounds and lift them on to the baking trays with a small palette knife. Prick each biscuit with a fork twice, and bake just above or in the centre of a pre-heated oven, at 300°F (mark 2), for about 25 minutes or until faintly tinged with brown. Cool on a wire rack and serve the biscuits dredged with caster sugar. Butter shorts will keep in a container for about 10 days.

Easter Biscuits

PREPARATION TIME: *35 min.*
COOKING TIME: *15–20 min.*

INGREDIENTS *(for 24 biscuits):*
4 oz. butter or block margarine
5 oz. caster sugar
1 egg
1 egg yolk
2 oz. currants
6 oz. plain flour
2 oz. rice flour
1 level teaspoon mixed spice
1–2 tablespoons milk

Line two or three baking trays with non-stick or buttered greaseproof paper. Cream the butter with a wooden spoon until soft, add 4 oz. of the sugar and beat thoroughly until pale and fluffy. Separate the egg and beat in the two egg yolks, and then stir in the currants. Sift the flours, together with the spice, into the creamed ingredients, a little at a time. Stir to combine, adding a little milk if necessary to bind the mixture to a soft but manageable dough.

Knead the dough lightly on a floured board, then roll it out $\frac{1}{8}$–$\frac{1}{4}$ in. thick. Cut into rounds with a $2\frac{1}{2}$ in. fluted cutter, and set the biscuits on the baking trays. Mark lines, about $\frac{1}{4}$ in. apart, with the back of a knife. Bake just above or in the centre of a pre-heated oven at 350°F (mark 4) for 15–20 minutes. After 10 minutes, brush the biscuits with the unbeaten egg white and dredge with the remaining sugar. Leave the biscuits to cool slightly, then lift on to a wire rack.

Serve while quite fresh.

PREPARED BISCUITS

These are usually round and thin, with a crisp texture. The soft dough is shaped into a long roll, wrapped in waxed, non-stick paper or kitchen foil and chilled for at least 2 hours. The roll is then cut into thin slices with a sharp knife and baked on greased baking trays. As the dough will keep for about 1 week in the refrigerator, the biscuits can be sliced and baked as required.

Refrigerator Cookies

PREPARATION TIME: *20 min.*
CHILLING TIME: *2 hours*
COOKING TIME: *10 min.*

INGREDIENTS *(for 48 biscuits):*
8 oz. plain flour
1 level teaspoon baking powder
5 oz. butter
6 oz. caster sugar or light, soft brown sugar
1 teaspoon vanilla essence
1 egg
2 oz. plain chocolate
2 oz. ground hazelnuts
Caster sugar for dusting

Sift together the flour and baking powder. Beat the butter with a wooden spoon until soft, add the sugar and continue beating until light and fluffy. Beat in the vanilla essence and the beaten egg. Add the flour, and grate the chocolate finely into the mixture; lastly add the nuts. Stir just enough to combine the ingredients. Shape the dough, on a lightly floured surface, into a sausage about 2 in. wide. Wrap in foil or paper, secure the ends and chill.

To bake the biscuits, slice off as many thin biscuits as required from the roll. Set them, well spaced out, on a greased baking tray. Sprinkle with sugar and bake in the centre of a pre-heated oven, at 375°F (mark 5), for about 10 minutes. Cool on a wire rack.

Biscuits/4

Confectionery/1

Chocolate fudge

Collettes

Coconut ice

Chocolate-covered dates

Chocolate-covered pineapple

Honey fruit nut caramels

Sweet-making is an absorbing hobby, and with practice and imagination the finished result looks temptingly professional. Home-made sweets, packed in decorative boxes, make ideal presents for Christmas and birthdays. Set the individual sweets in paper cases and put waxed paper between the layers.

Many traditional sweets, such as fudge and toffee, are based on concentrated sugar syrup, boiled to high temperatures. A cooking thermometer and a large, heavy-based pan are essential. Use a wooden spoon when needed, to move the mixture backwards and forwards while the syrup is reducing. The thermometer should be moved occasionally, as fudge and toffee tend to settle round the bulb and give inaccurate readings.

For chocolate-covered sweets, use good-quality plain chocolate. Put it, broken into small pieces, in a bowl and set this over a pan of hot water. Stir the chocolate continuously with a fork until melted – it should be just warm and must never be allowed to boil. Dip the sweets, one at a time, into the chocolate, holding each between two forks, and brush off any excess on the side of the bowl. Leave the sweets to set on non-stick or waxed paper.

Chocolate Fudge

PREPARATION TIME: *about 1 hour*

INGREDIENTS *(for 1½ lb.)*:
1 lb. caster sugar
½ pint water
1 large tin condensed milk
4½ oz. chocolate dots or plain cooking chocolate (grated)
2 oz. seedless raisins (optional)

Put the sugar and water in a heavy-based 6 pint pan and dissolve the sugar over low heat. Bring to the boil, add the condensed milk and boil gently until the thermometer registers 240°F. Stir occasionally to prevent sticking. Remove the pan from the heat and add the chocolate, and raisins if used.

Beat the mixture until thick and creamy, using a wooden spoon; pour it into a buttered tin, about 5½ in. by 8 in. by 1 in.

Leave to cool for several hours, then cut the fudge into 1 in. squares with a sharp knife. Wrap in waxed paper.

Collettes

PREPARATION TIME: *1 hour*

INGREDIENTS *(for 18)*:
9 oz. chocolate dots
4 tablespoons strong black coffee
2 oz. butter
2 egg yolks
Rum
Blanched hazel nuts

Melt 4 oz. of the chocolate dots. Cool slightly, then put a teaspoon of the melted chocolate into a small paper sweet case; press another case over the chocolate to squeeze it up the sides. Repeat with the remaining chocolate. Leave overnight.

The next day, peel off the paper cases. Melt the remaining chocolate dots as before, and stir in the coffee. When cool, beat in the softened, but not oily, butter and the egg yolks; add rum to taste. Spoon this mixture into a forcing bag fitted with a large star nozzle and pipe into the chocolate cases. Top each collette with a hazelnut and leave to set.

Coconut Ice

PREPARATION TIME: *30 min.*

INGREDIENTS *(for 24–30)*:
1 lb. caster sugar
¼ pint milk
5 oz. desiccated coconut
Cochineal

Oil or butter a shallow tin, 8 in. by 6 in. Dissolve the sugar in the milk over low heat, then bring to the boil and boil gently for about 10 minutes or until the temperature reaches 240°F (read the thermometer at eye level). Remove the pan from the heat and stir in the coconut.

Pour half the mixture quickly into the tin, spreading it evenly. Colour the remainder pale pink with a few drops of cochineal and pour quickly over the first layer. Leave until half-set, then mark the coconut into 1 in. squares with a knife. Cut up when quite cold.

Chocolate-covered Dates

PREPARATION TIME: *20 min.*

INGREDIENTS:
1 box dates
Almond paste
4 oz. plain chocolate
Cocktail cherries
Shelled walnuts

Using a small, pointed knife, make a small slit in each date and remove the stone. Fill the cavities with plain almond paste and close the dates again. Melt the chocolate in a bowl over a pan of hot water and, with the aid of two forks, dip the dates in the chocolate. Coat evenly and brush off any surplus on the edge of the bowl.

Dry the chocolate-covered dates on sheets of waxed or non-stick paper. Just before set, decorate the dates with well-drained cocktail cherries cut in half or with pieces of shelled walnuts.

Chocolate-covered Pineapple

PREPARATION TIME: *20 min.*

INGREDIENTS:
Small tin pineapple rings
6–7 oz. plain chocolate
Decorations

Drain the pineapple rings thoroughly and cut them into halves or quarters. Break up the chocolate and melt in a bowl over a pan of hot water. Using two forks, carefully dip the pineapple chunks in the chocolate, coating them evenly.

Dry on waxed or non-stick paper, and before the chocolate sets, decorate with crystallised violets, yellow mimosa balls or silver dragees.

Honey Fruit Nut Caramels

PREPARATION TIME: *30 min.*

INGREDIENTS:
3 oz. butter
5 oz. golden syrup
6 oz. clear honey
4 oz. walnut halves
4 oz. stoned dates

Grease and line with non-stick paper a shallow tin measuring 8 in. by 5 in. Melt the butter in a large, heavy-based pan set over low heat; add the syrup and honey. Bring the mixture to the boil and continue boiling over gentle heat until the thermometer registers 270°F. Meanwhile, chop the walnuts and dates finely.

Remove the pan from the heat and add the nuts and dates. Beat the mixture vigorously with a wooden spoon until opaque in colour. Pour it into the tin and leave to cool. When almost set, cut through the caramel with a buttered knife, into $\frac{3}{4}$–1 in. squares. Leave to set for about 24 hours, then break the squares apart; wrap them in waxed paper and store.

Marzipan Confectionery
INGREDIENTS:
Almond paste or marzipan
Food colouring
Almonds
Granulated sugar
Dates
Plain chocolate for melting
Stem ginger

Cooked almond paste or bought marzipan is popular for many sweets. The almond paste may be coloured pink, green or yellow with a little food colouring, and used as a base or filling for sweets.

Stuffed dates: make a slit in the top of the dates and remove the stones. Fill the cavities with a small piece of plain or coloured almond paste; roll the stuffed dates in granulated sugar or decorate them with blanched almonds.

Ginger marzipan: shape pieces of almond paste into marble-sized balls, dip the bases in melted chocolate and top with well-drained pieces of stem ginger.

Peanut Brittle
PREPARATION TIME: *1 hour*

INGREDIENTS:
12 oz. loaf or cube sugar
$\frac{1}{4}$ pint water
$\frac{1}{2}$ lb. golden syrup
2 level teaspoons powdered glucose
1 oz. butter
3 oz. browned peanuts
$\frac{1}{2}$ teaspoon lemon essence
2 level teaspoons bicarbonate of soda

Dissolve the sugar in the water, together with the syrup and glucose, in a large, heavy-based pan set over low heat. Bring to the boil and boil gently until the thermometer registers 300°F (read at eye level).

Add the butter, warmed nuts (rub the skins off first) and lemon essence; heat until the butter is just melted. Stir in the bicarbonate of soda (the mixture will froth rapidly for a few minutes), and pour it quickly on to an oiled marble slab or large clean baking tray.

When cold, break the brittle into pieces; store in single layers between waxed or non-stick paper.

Peppermint Creams
PREPARATION TIME: *30 min.*

INGREDIENTS *(for 25)*:
8 oz. icing sugar
1 egg white
Peppermint essence

Sift the icing sugar into a bowl and blend with enough beaten egg white to form a stiff paste. Add a few drops of peppermint essence to taste.

Knead the paste lightly in the bowl, using the fingertips. Roll the paste out $\frac{1}{4}$ in. thick, between sheets of non-stick or waxed paper. Stamp out 1 in. rounds with a plain cutter, and leave the mints to dry for about 24 hours.

Rum Truffles
PREPARATION TIME: *35 min.*
CHILLING TIME: *1 hour*

INGREDIENTS *(for 12)*:
3 oz. plain chocolate
1 egg yolk
$\frac{1}{2}$ oz. butter
1 teaspoon rum
1 teaspoon top of the milk or single cream
2 oz. chocolate vermicelli or drinking chocolate

Melt the chocolate in a small bowl over a pan of hot water. Add the egg yolk, butter, rum and milk. Beat the mixture until thick, then chill in the refrigerator until firm enough to handle.

Shape the mixture into 12 balls and toss at once in vermicelli or drinking chocolate.

Iced Petits Fours
PREPARATION TIME: *$1\frac{1}{4}$ hours*
COOKING TIME: *30 min.*

INGREDIENTS *(for 24–30 cakes)*:
3 large eggs
3 oz. caster sugar
$2\frac{1}{2}$ oz. plain flour
1 level tablespoon cornflour
$1\frac{1}{2}$ oz. unsalted butter
Apricot glaze
1 lb. almond paste
Glacé icing (from 1 lb. icing sugar)
Food colourings
Flavourings (optional)
Decorations

Grease and base-line a rectangular tin, 1 in. deep by 10 in. by 6 in. Make up the eggs, sugar, flours and butter as described for Genoese sponge. Turn the mixture into the tin, levelling the top evenly, and bake just above the centre of a pre-heated oven, at 375°F (mark 5), for about 30 minutes. Turn out to cool on a covered wire rack and remove the lining paper.

Cut the sponge, on a flat surface, into 24–30 small shapes, such as squares, diamonds, rounds and crescents. Brush the petits fours with warm apricot glaze, and roll out the almond paste thinly. Cut the paste into the same type of shapes as the petits fours and lay them over the brushed cakes.

Make up the glacé icing into a coating consistency, divide it into four portions and colour three of these green, pink or lemon. Flavouring may be added to match each colour. Set the petits fours on a wire tray over a plate and carefully spoon the icing over the cakes, using a teaspoon and letting the icing run down the sides. When the icing is nearly set, decorate the cakes with, for example, glacé cherries, angelica, mimosa balls, silver dragees, nuts, or crystallised violets and rose petals.

Almond Petits Fours
PREPARATION TIME: *20 min.*
COOKING TIME: *20 min.*

INGREDIENTS *(for 24–30 cakes)*:
2 egg whites
4 oz. ground almonds
2 oz. caster sugar
Almond essence
Rice paper
Glacé cherries
Angelica

Line two or three baking trays with rice paper. Whisk the egg whites in a deep bowl until stiff; lightly fold in the almonds and sugar and add a few drops of almond essence.

Spoon the mixture into a forcing bag fitted with a large rose vegetable nozzle and pipe it on to the baking trays in small rosettes and 'S' shapes. Decorate the petits fours with glacé cherries or strips of angelica.

Bake in the centre of a pre-heated oven, at 350°F (mark 4), for about 20 minutes or until golden brown.

Confectionery/2

Marzipan confectionery

Peanut brittle

Peppermint creams

Rum truffles

Iced petits fours

Almond petits fours

Index

Bold type indicates chapter headings and colour illustrations